Moving

To The Next Level

Becoming a Fully-Developing Follower of Christ

Pastor John D. Ogletree, Jr.

Moving To The Next Level

Becoming A Fully-Developing Follower of Christ

Copyright © 2001 John D. Ogletree, Jr.

ISBN 1-891773-26-7

Published by

Orman Press

4200 Sandy Lake Drive

Lithonia, GA 30038

T. 770.808.0999

F. 770.808.1955

E-mail: Ormanmcc@aol.com

http://www.Ormanpress.com

Dedication

This book is dedicated to the loving memory of my father, Reverend John D. Ogletree, Sr.; to my mother, Marion Deckard who instilled the Christian faith in me at an early age; my lovely, devoted wife Evelyn of 28, years; my oldest son Reverend Johnny III and his wife Quinita; my grandchildren, Layla and Elianah; my beautiful daughter, Lambreni, my two younger sons, Joseph and Jordan, and the First Metropolitan Church where I joyfully serve as Senior Pastor.

Foreword
by Dr. George O. McCalep

There is a buzz phrase moving like the wind across the body of Christ (the Church). The buzz praise is "next level." Everybody, including many secular corporations are dialoging and strategizing about moving to the next level. Dr. John Ogletree's book that bears the title *Moving To The Next Level* explores the dynamics of the phenomenal movement as it relates to the church. Through an inspiring sermonic style of writing, Dr. Ogletree explains the biblical meaning and process of moving to the next level. He straightforthly deals with the critical issue of becoming a fully-developing follower of Christ. In every chapter, he encourages and admonishes the reader to move to the next level of spiritual development in areas such as praise and prayer. The book is theologically sound, but also very practical. The practical aspect is rooted in the author's character and accomplishments. Dr. Ogletree is an attorney called by God to be a pastor whose ministry can be described as cutting-edge. I have had the privilege and pleasure to visit the First Metropolitan Baptist Church in Houston, Texas on many occasions. This is where Dr. Ogletree has pastored for the past 15 years. I can bear witness to the fact that he practices what he preaches. His ministry can definitely be described as a "next level" ministry.

Table of Contents

1

Next Level Prayer

1 Chronicles 4:9-10 NIV

9 Jabez was more honorable than his brothers. His mother named him Jabez saying, "I gave birth to him in pain."

10 Jabez cried out to the God of Israel, "Oh that you would bless me and enlarge my territory. Let your hand be with me and keep me from harm so that I will be free from pain." And God granted his request.

Have you ever wondered why some people are able to rise above the rest? Why are some able to rise above poverty, racism, abandonment, divorce, abuse, disability, loneliness, grief, a broken heart, betrayal, failure, addiction and even the demonic? Why are some able to reach levels of radical riches? Why do some people seem to always have the respect of their peers? Why are some people always receiving a blessing from God? They seem to always rendez-vous with righteous rewards. When they get in trouble, it seems like God quickly sends the angels to get them out. We know that the Lord has a reward for the righteous, but they seem to always be blessed on another level. Two verses in 1 Chronicles provide a simple answer: next level prayer.

What Is Next Level Prayer?

Next level prayer is prayer that dares to trust God to liberate as well as lift the believer from the circumstances of the past and present so that they can be used by God.

What Must Be Considered?

As believers, we know that God does not show favoritism toward any of His children. What He so willingly does for one, He will do for the other. We are taught in scripture that, *"For God does not show favoritism"* (Romans 2:11 NIV). But we wonder and want to know why some seem to prosper so far beyond the rest. There are some common assumptions that many of us make when we see the continuous flow of blessings others experience. Often we say it's luck. We attribute their consistent fortune to luck and actually begin to hope for the same luck ourselves. And if we don't count luck as the source, we might say it's hard work. We think in our minds, "Ah, they work harder. They burn that midnight oil. They put in fourteen hours a day and the person who works fourteen hours, is going to get ahead." And if it's not luck or hard work, the next assumption we make is that it's long-study. Or, some people believe it's family or friends. And in some cases, we believe it's their money or fate, that some people were just destined to be rich and have a big and prosperous lifestyle.

In 1 Chronicles 4:9-10, we are told of Jabez, a man who was given a name meaning "pain or sorrow" by his mother at his birth. She labeled him. In Old Testament times, names were given based on an individual's qualities or the circumstances surrounding their birth. The birth of Jabez must have been so troublesome and so dramatic that his mother labeled him because of what she experienced or felt.

Like many believers today, Jabez's labeling from birth must have left a lingering psychological mark on him as a child. In spite of his labeling, the Word of God says that *"Jabez was more honorable than his brothers" (1 Chronicles 4:9 NIV)* which leads us to believe that Jabez did not live out the qualities associated with his name. He was not a man who by the mere mention of his name others were reminded of the great pain and sorrow his name stood for. But instead, he was a man of character. If children of God are to experience the blessings of next level prayer, we must be people of character. We must develop a strong character and know that our labels, like that of Jabez do not define us.

However, many times we are unable to overcome the negative labels that are placed upon us as children. Consequently, we begin to act out openly the negative tendencies associated with our labels. Jabez recognized that he could not change his past so he decided to change his destiny. He understood what he could not do and reconciled what he could do - he could go to God in prayer. And like Jabez, none of us can change our pasts - how we were brought up, that we were raised in the projects around crime and drugs, or that our parents were alcoholics - but we can change our destinies. If we are actively involved in prayer and believe that prayer changes things, and nothing is changing, it must be how we're praying. Through next level prayer, Jabez was able to overcome. Jabez prayed and what he could not change, he placed before God and allowed Him to transform his destiny. Next level prayer will change things. The blessings Jabez experienced as a result of his prayer teach us that the reason some people rise above the rest is prayer. Your prayer life can cause you to rise above the rest. Jabez moved up, not because of luck, hard work, fate, long-study, family, friends or money. Just as a fully-developing follower of Christ moves up, he moved up because of prayer. Next level prayer is a choice.

Next level prayer is a choice.

You must long for more. Jabez longed for more. Verse 10 reads, *"Jabez cried out to the God of Israel, 'Oh that you would bless me and enlarge my territory. Let your hand be with me and keep me from harm so that I will be free from pain.'"* Just as Jabez was discontent, believers must also be discontent if we are going to bring about change in our lives through prayer. God answers sincere and earnest prayers. Contentment, or a lack of desire for change, will not produce next level results. Nor does it promote growth in the life of the believer. We should desire to be free from bondage, fear, oppression and fruitless living. We must become dissatisfied with prayers that do not produce the break-throughs we need in our lives. Growth and continued development should always be at work in the life of believers. As we mature and achieve new levels of development in our prayer lives, fear should not be an acceptable response when we are called on to pray, or when we know we should witness to an unbeliever. We must not be satisfied with sitting Sunday after Sunday in the worship service and not

Contentment, or a lack of desire for change, will not produce next level results.

serving the Lord and His church any other times. We must long for more. Contentment, or a lack of desire for change, will not produce next level results.

You must look in the right direction. Many believers want to experience abundant blessings in their lives but fail to go to God who is the source of all blessings. The Word of God instructs us that *"Every good and perfect gift is from above, coming down from the Father of the heavenly lights, who does not change like shifting shadows" (James 1:17 NIV).*

Next level prayer must be directed to God. Jabez fervently cried out to God. And the scripture refers to God as *"the God of Israel"* which says that Jabez knew God to be a

Deliverer, as He had delivered Israel from bondage. He acknowledged God as the source of his deliverance. We must cry out to God knowing that He is our true source of help. We must be persistent like the psalmist who wrote, *"I will lift up my eyes to the hills - where does my help come from? My help comes from the Lord, the Maker of heaven and earth" (Psalm 121:1-2 NIV),* and, *"But I call to God, and the Lord saves me" (Psalm 55:16 NIV).* We must be careful not to look for abundance in the wrong places.

> *We must be careful not to look for abundance in the wrong places.*

You must make your desires known to God. Jabez made his desires known to God. We should not be afraid to approach God with our deepest concerns. Jabez looked to God in faith, hope and belief that He could change his situation. Now the truth of the matter is that God already knew Jabez's needs. In spite of God's omniscience, He would still have us freely and openly come to Him in prayer. He may not grant our request every time, but He wants us to be confident that we can come to Him. The scripture declares, *"Let us then approach the*

> *In spite of God's omniscience, He would still have us freely and openly come to Him in prayer.*

13

throne of grace with confidence, so that we may receive mercy and find grace to help us in our time of need" (Hebrews 4:16 NIV).

Where Does God Want Me To Be?

Prioritize your spiritual development. We must be mindful that our spiritual development is God's priority. Jabez asked that God would bless him spiritually. What is key about spiritual blessings is that they are not solely for the benefit of the person making the request, but they also include others. As we begin to make our personal growth and maturity our greatest desire, we will experience the willingness of God to answer our requests.

Request the expansion of your boundaries. Jabez requested that God would reposition his limitations. If we feel limited in any area of our lives, we can ask God and He can expand our boundaries. We can only experience an expansion beyond our own limitations through prayer. We cannot operate outside of our limitations by ourselves. But through next level prayer and the help of God, we can exceed our own abilities.

Seek additional influence. With expansion comes greater influence. When God expands our boundaries, we are ultimately asking for the opportunity to perform additional service, so that others can be impacted. The purpose of the expansion, whether it be spiritual or material, is so that someone will be drawn to a God who hears, cares and acts on behalf of the lost, least and the last.

Recognize the sustaining power of God. Jabez asked for God's continued power and provision in his life. He says, *"Let your hand be with me."* He knew that he needed to depend on God, after God expanded His boundaries, for his continued sufficiency. He did not foolishly think that he could operate apart from God. If the blessing came from God's hand, it would take God's hand to maintain it. We must also ask God to sustain us in the midst of our blessings. Next level prayer recognizes the need for God in light of our blessings and seeks the continued abiding of God's hand in our lives. It also asks for God's continued provision and power in our lives.

Finally, we have God's response to this next level prayer: "And God granted his request."

Study Guide: Moving To Next Level Prayer

1. Jabez means _____ or _____.

2. Next level prayer is a _____.

3. _____ , or a lack of desire for change, will not produce next level results.

4. We must be careful not to look for _____ in the
   wrong places.

5. What are some of the false assumptions we make regarding the reason for the success others experience:

   a. _____
   b. _____
   c. _____
   d. _____
   e. _____
   f. _____
   g. _____

6. God wants you to:

     a. _____ your spiritual development

     b. _____ the expansion of your boundaries

     c. _____ additional influence

     d. _____ the sustaining power of God

7. What do the following verses share about next level prayer?

    Hebrews 7:19

    Ephesians 3:12

    1 John 3:21

8. Scripture Memory: Philippians 4:6

2

Next Level Purity

Matthew 5:20 NIV

20 For I tell you that unless your righteousness surpasses that of the Pharisees
and the teachers of the law, you will certainly not enter the kingdom of heaven.

How many believers are conscious of the fact that their lives must be acceptable to God? Often, we spend a lot of time trying to gain acceptance on our jobs, in our communities, fraternities, sororities or other civic organizations, but the truth is that we need to be acceptable to God.

What Is Next Level Purity?

Next level purity refers to integrity, virtue, purity of life, correctness of thinking, feeling and behavior. It is the condition of being acceptable to God.

What Must Be Considered?

During the ministry of Christ, the Scribes and Pharisees were seen as models of righteousness and purity. The strict obedience to the law that they imposed on themselves and others was their measure of being in right relationship with God. They sought to follow the law in its entirety. They were held in high esteem and respected as people who were living pure and righteous lives. In light of this, Jesus said to people who felt that there was no way to measure up to the Scribes and Pharisees, *"unless your righteousness surpasses that of the Pharisees and the teachers of the law."* Jesus challenges them to move to a level above not just equal to the Scribes and Pharisees but beyond their mark. The Greek word for surpass

or exceed means to excel, to abound or overflow. But He is
not referring to more rules, ceremonies, rituals or tradition.
It's a righteousness of the heart. Next level purity involves the
heart of the believer. There were many problems with the
righteousness of the Scribes and Pharisees.

It was external. Jesus says that they loved to clean the
outside of the dish, but inside, they were full of wickedness.
They majored in all the exterior things that others could plainly see. Jesus speaks to this in Luke when He says, *"Then the
Lord said to him, Now then, you Pharisees clean the outside
of the cup and dish, but inside you are full of greed and
wickedness" (Luke 11:39 NIV).*

It was burdensome. They were trying to live out all of
the 613 rabbinical laws, and were placing the same stipulation
for purity on others. The scripture records, *"The teachers of
the law and the Pharisees sit in Moses' seat. So you must obey
them and do everything they tell you. But do not do what they
do, for they do not practice what they preach. They tie up
heavy loads and put them on men's shoulders, but they themselves are not willing to lift a finger to move them" (Matthew
23:2-4 NIV).*

It was selective. They majored in purity in one area and
minored in it in others. They picked and chose what portion

of God's law they were going to obey and disregarded the rest. Jesus says, *"Woe to you, teachers of the law and Pharisees, you hypocrites! You give a tenth of your spices - mint, dill and cummin. But you have neglected the more important matters of the law - justice, mercy and faithfulness. You should have practiced the latter, without neglecting the former"* *(Matthew 23:23 NIV)*. In order to achieve purity through the law, one must obey all of the law. If you break one, you break all of them. So we cannot be selective as Christians. We are to obey the total will and Word of God.

It was self-exalting. Jesus shared their self-exalting nature in a parable focusing on a Pharisee and a tax collector when He told the disciples to pray and not faint. *"The Pharisee stood up and prayed about himself: 'God, I thank you that I am not like other men - robbers, evildoers, adulterers - or even like this tax collector'"* *(Luke 18:11 NIV)*. Believers in Christ are not to exalt themselves above others. In fact, we are taught *"but in humility consider others better than ourselves"* *(Philippians 2:3b NIV)*. We are to exalt Christ and in our humbleness to the Lord, He will lift us up.

It was hypocritical. In Mark 7:6, Jesus says that Isaiah was right when he prophesied about them in that they honored Him with their lips, but their hearts were far from God. Their religion was for the purpose of being seen of men. *"He replied, "Isaiah was right when he prophesied about you hypocrites; as it is written: "'These people honor me with their lips, but their hearts are far from me. They worship me in vain; their teachings are but rules taught by men'"* (Mark 7:6-7 NIV).

It was negative. They were looking for fault in others because their righteousness was based on what you could not do. As believers we must be careful not to fall into the same trap of negativity. We must learn to focus on the liberation we have been given in the Lord instead of the restrictions placed in some areas within our lives. For the Word of God says, *"Now the Lord is the Spirit, and where the Spirit of the Lord is, there is freedom"* (2 Corinthians 3:17 NIV).

It was deficient. In not keeping with God's will, the Scribes failed to produce fruit in their lives. They did not fulfill God's intent. Their purity was also deficient in that it did not follow the spirit of the law. God knows that we are unable to gain righteousness through our works. As a witness for Christ, if we possess a condescending attitude and a judgmental spirit, we will never make a positive, Christ-like impact on the lives of those around us.

It did not give God glory. Because God's intent was not

fulfilled in the practices of the Scribes and Pharisees, He was not glorified. The manifestation of God's power was not perfected in the lives of the Scribes and Pharisees as they sought to live the total law.

The purity that God has made available to His children through Jesus Christ is not bound in the same legalism of the Scribes and Pharisees. Next level purity embraces believers being the salt of the earth which Christ spoke of in Matthew 5:13. We are to bring others to Christ through our sincere witness and lifestyle in the Lord. Our lifestyle should be attractive to non-believers and not unrealistic.

Next level purity must be rooted in the right attitude. Believers must possess the right attitude toward God, His Word and other people. Christ details this righteousness in Matthew 5:28-48 NIV: *"But I tell you that anyone who looks at a woman lustfully has already committed adultery with her in his heart. If your right eye causes you to sin, gouge it out and throw it away. It is better for you to lose one part of your body than for your whole body to be thrown into hell. And if your right hand causes you to sin, cut it off and throw it away. It is better for you to lose one part of your body than for your whole body to go into hell. "It has been said, 'Anyone who divorces his wife must give her a certificate of divorce.' But I tell you that anyone who divorces his wife, except for marital unfaithfulness, causes her to become an adulteress, and anyone who marries the divorced woman commits adultery.*

"Again, you have heard that it was said to the people long ago, 'Do not break your oath, but keep the oaths you have made to the Lord.' But I tell you, Do not swear at all: either by heaven, for it is God's throne; or by the earth, for it is his footstool; or by Jerusalem, for it is the city of the Great King. And do not swear by your head, for you cannot make even one hair white or black. Simply let your 'Yes' be 'Yes,' and your 'No,' 'No'; anything beyond this comes from the evil one.

"You have heard that it was said, 'Eye for eye, and tooth for tooth.' But I tell you, Do not resist an evil person. If someone strikes you on the right cheek, turn to him the other also. And if someone wants to sue you and take your tunic, let him have your cloak as well. If someone forces you to go one mile, go with him two miles. Give to the one who asks you, and do not turn away from the one who wants to borrow from you. "You have heard that it was said, 'Love your neighbor and hate your enemy.' But I tell you: Love your enemies and pray for those who persecute you, that you may be sons of your Father in heaven. He causes his sun to rise on the evil and the good, and sends rain on the righteous and the unrighteous. If you

love those who love you, what reward will you get? Are not even the tax collectors doing that? And if you greet only your brothers, what are you doing more than others? Do not even pagans do that? Be perfect, therefore, as your heavenly Father is perfect." In these verses of scripture, Jesus stresses having a right attitude toward God, His Word and other people. This attitude intends to fulfill God's will, seeks to follow the Spirit of God's Word, produces the fruit of purity and gives glory to God.

The purity that believers are to possess, next level righteousness:

Reverences life. In Matthew 5:21 Jesus teaches on the topic of murder. He first reminds the disciples that the law forbids it. But He takes murder to a new level when He says that through hatred, we commit murder in our hearts. The righteousness of God looks first at the heart of man. It is an inward righteousness. A fully-developing follower of Jesus Christ is to appreciate his new life in Christ and have respect for the lives of others.

Prioritizes reconciliation with others. Next level purity understands that people are important to God. Consequently, our relationship with others is important to God. We are taught in Matthew 5:23 of the necessity of reconciliation before we can make an acceptable offering to God. *"Therefore if thou bring thy gift to the altar, and there rememberest that thy brother hath aught against thee"* *(Matthew 5:23 NIV).* It is more important to be reconciled with others than to participate in religious duties.

> *It is more important to be reconciled with others than to participate in religious duties.*

Hates sin. In light of God's focus on the heart of man, Jesus illustrates the need for believers to hate sin so much so that we would rather lose limb than eternal life. *"If your right eye causes you to sin, gouge it out and throw it away. It is better for you to lose one part of your body than for your whole body to be thrown into hell"* *(Matthew 5:29 NIV).*

Is committed to marriage and family. In Matthew 5:27, Jesus gives insight on the topic of adultery. He says that anyone who divorces his wife for any other reason than unfaithfulness commits adultery. He goes back to the fact that the Father's original intent for marriage was that men and women would remain together. Matthew 19:6 NIV reads, *"So they are no longer two, but one. Therefore what God has joined together, let man not separate."*

Is honest. At that time, it was common for people to swear by their statements in the effort to give them greater credibility. Jesus shares with the disciples that the word of the believer should be sufficient. If we are practicing honesty, we do no need to swear by the Bible, anyone's grave or our lives. We should have a reputation of being people of our word.

Accepts suffering. The thought of suffering is not a pleasant one. But suffering for Christ's sake is part of the next level purity God has for us. The old school of thought was consistent with the "eye for an eye" teaching. But in Matthew 5:38-42, Jesus dispels that thought with a new one requiring the believer to endure hardship, just as Christ did. *"You have heard that is was said, 'Eye for eye, and tooth for tooth.' But I tell you, Do not resist an evil person. If someone strikes you on the right cheek, turn to him the other also. and if someone wants to sue you and take your tunic, let him have your cloak as well. If someone forces you to go one mile, go with him two miles. Give to the one who asks you, and do not turn away from the one who wants to borrow from you"* (Matthew 5:38-42 NIV).

Involves sacrificial love. We are called not only to love those who love us, but also those who do not. The test of our purity is if we can love those who dislike us, hate us, and even try and hurt us. When we love, we are most like God. He demonstrated His love for us when He gave His Son, Jesus

28

Christ, to die for our sins. *Matthew 5:43-48 NIV: "You have heard that it was said, 'Love your neigh-bor and hate your enemy.' But I tell you: Love your enemies and pray for those who persecute you, that you may be sons of your Father in heaven. He causes his sun to rise on the evil and the good, and sends rain on the righteous and the unrighteous.*

> *The test of our righteousness is if we can love those who dislike us, hate us, and even try and hurt us.*

If you love those who love you, what reward will you get? Are not even the tax collectors doing that? And if you greet only your brothers, what are you doing more than others? Do not even pagans doing that? Be perfect, therefore, as your heavenly Father is perfect."

Where Does God Want Me To Be?

First, purity begins with faith in Jesus Christ. Paul wrote to the Roman church that righteousness from God comes through faith to all who believe. The acceptance of Jesus Christ makes purity a reality in our lives.

Second, as we experience more of Christ in our lives, practice humility. A major downfall in the purity of the Scribes and Pharisees is that they were proud. They were not humble toward God as they sought to please Him. As a fully-developing follower of Christ, we must remember that grace is still an operative word in our lives. Grace is not only necessary when we receive Christ, it is also necessary post-salvation. God would not have us to be full of pride. In fact, Proverbs 6:16-17 teaches us that a proud look is an abomination to the Lord. We must be humble so that Satan will not take advantage of us because of pride.

Third, we are to be active in living the Word of God. James 1:22 NIV reads, *"Do not merely listen to the word, and so deceive yourselves. Do what it says."*

As disciples, it is not enough for us to only hear the Word of God preached. If we are to achieve next level righteousness, we must not fall victim to deception of being only good listeners, but instead, we must apply it to our daily lives. The Word

> *The Word of God is intended to be more than the forty-five minute sermon we experience each Sunday.*

of God is intended to be more than the forty-five minute sermon we experience each Sunday.

Fourth, we need to empathize with others. Witnessing concerning the salvation of Jesus Christ is necessary for every maturing believer. Because we were at one time without Christ, we should never judge the actions of others. If we are to walk in next level purity, even though we may not have direct experience with the same situation someone else may be going through, we most certainly can relate to committing an act outside of God's will. Part of what makes our witness effective is our ability to emphathize with those who do not know Christ as their personal Lord and Savior. We must be reminded of Romans 3:23 which states that *"for all have sinned and fall short of the glory of God."* And Galatians 6:1 further supports our need to

> *Part of what makes our witness effective is our ability to emphathize with those who do not know Christ as their personal Lord and Savior.*

empathize by telling us, *"Brothers, if someone is caught in a sin, you who are spiritual should restore him gently. But watch yourself, or you also may be tempted."*

And, finally in our pursuit of next level purity is confession. Believers need to always practice repentance. We are to confess our sins. We should not reach a point in our walk with the Lord when we think that we know everything or are incapable of sinning. When we confess our sins, God is faithful and just to forgive us and to cleanse us from all unrighteousness (1 John 1:9 NIV).

Study Guide: Moving To Next Level Purity

1. Next level purity is not to be like the righteousness of the Scribes and Pharisees. It is NOT supposed to be:

    a. _____ Luke 11:39

    b. _____ Matthew 23:2-4

    c. _____ Matthew 23:23

    d. _____ Luke 18:11

    e. _____ Mark 7:6

    f. _____ Mark 2:24

2. It is more important to be _____ with others than to participate in religious duties.

3. Next level purity:

    a. _____

    b. _____

    c. _____

    d. _____

    e. _____

4. _____ begins with faith in Jesus Christ.

5. As we experience more of Christ in our lives, we are to practice _____.

6. We are to be active in _____ the Word of God.

7. We need to _____ with others.

8. Believers need to always practice _____.

9. The Word of God is _____ to be more than a forty-five minute sermon we experience each Sunday.

10. Part of what makes our _____ effective is our ability to empathize with those who do not know Christ as their personal Lord and Savior.

11. The test of our righteousness is if we can love those who _____ us, hate us, and even try and hurt us.

12. What do the following verses share about next level purity?

    2 Corinthians 6:14

Romans 5:17

1 Corinthians 15:34

13. Scripture Memory: Romans 6:13

3

Next Level Power

John 14:12 NIV

12 I tell you the truth, anyone who has faith in me will do what I've been doing. He will do even greater things than these because I am going to the Father.

In the 14th chapter of John, Jesus shares his approaching departure with his disciples. He encourages them not to allow their hearts to become troubled. The disciples are more than likely confused and sadness begins to set in among them as Jesus talks about his pending departure. It is then that Christ reassures them that His departure does not bring their work to an end. In fact, He says that they will continue in the work they had begun together and go on to do even greater works.

What prevents many believers from accomplishing the "greater works" Christ spoke of in John 14? If we are to become fully-developing followers of Christ, we must recognize the power He intended for us to have. His death was dreadful, but necessary, so that He might resurrect in victory over sin and death. His resurrection secured power for those who would believe on His name. His resurrection was one of power to which we also, as believers, may have access.

What Is Next Level Power?

Next level power is the fulfillment of the Holy Spirit in the life of the believer who is actively working in their God-given ministry.

What Must Be Considered?

Every believer has the potential to succeed in the plan

God has for them. We can claim the promises of God as our own. These promises include a promise of potential. *"I tell you the truth, anyone who has faith in me will do what I have been doing. He will do even greater things than these, because I am going to the Father," (John 14:12 NIV).* Jesus said we could do greater works. Greater works than Christ? This seems impossible. The disciples were no doubt wondering how they were going to be able to accomplish greater works than the Master. And not only the disciples, but every believer has been given this same potential to succeed. Jesus did not expect his disciples to disband after his departure. His promise that they would do the same works He had done and even greater works, was yet to be fulfilled. The word in the text, "greater" in the Greek is *meizon* which means "larger, more." We remember that Jesus turned water into wine, healed the sick, and raised the dead. So when the time came for Jesus to compare the work of the believer with the miracles He performed during His time with His disciples, Christ says we will do "greater works."

The temptation exists for believers today to think that the "greater" Jesus spoke of only applies to the original twelve disciples who actually walked alongside Him during His earthly ministry. They were the ones He was speaking directly to at that time, but that was not what Jesus intended to communicate to them or present-day believers. The qualification necessary to claim the promise of the potential, of the greater works Christ spoke of, is solely to be a believer. Next level power is available to every believer.

Once the disciples understood their potential, it was then that Jesus taught them about the source of their power to do these works. He taught them about the Holy Spirit. *"If you love me, you will obey what I command. And I will ask the Father, and he will give you another Counselor to be with you forever -" (John 14:15-16 NIV).* Jesus' departure was necessary so that the Holy Spirit would come. In light of His relationship with the Father, which He openly and intimately shared with the disciples and others He came in contact with, Jesus uses the Father's commitment to Him as a point of reference to model the level of commitment He possessed for His followers. The same commitment the Father has to the Son, the Son has to anyone who believes. As Christ demonstrated His commitment on Calvary, the promised Holy Spirit is the fulfillment of that commitment. Moving to the next level can only occur when we willingly decide not to operate in our own power,

> *Next level power is available to every believer.*

strength, or knowledge. We were never intended to operate in the body of Christ on anything less than the power He provides in the person of the Holy Spirit.

The Greek translation for the Holy Spirit is *parakletos* meaning "called to one's side." He is an intercessor and advocate for believers with the Father. He is not just for charismatic and Pentecostal believers, but rather He is for the church - for all believers. Because the Holy Spirit was given to the church after the ascension

> *We were never intended to operate in the body of Christ on anything less than the power He provides in the person of the Holy Spirit.*

of Jesus in replace of Christ, the word for "another" in the text, *allos*, in the Greek means "another of the same kind." The Holy Spirit, the church's provision for next level power, is Christ without the limitations of the flesh. Thus, what God is proposing to do in our lives, is to take us beyond fleshly limitations. It is the Holy Spirit who makes possible the greater works Christ spoke of before His departure. His presence has purpose; it is permanent; it is personal. *"But the Counselor, the Holy Spirit, whom the Father will send in my name, will teach you all things and will remind you of everything I have said to you" (John 14:26 NIV).*

The Holy Spirit also is our teacher. He will teach us

everything we need to know in order to carry out our function in the work of the ministry. And not only that, He will teach us in all areas of our lives - how to be a father, how to be a mother, how to be a wife, how to be a husband, how to be a parent, how to be a minister, how to be a devotional leader, how to be a deacon - whatever our needs are, the Holy Spirit will direct us in the truth.

Despite the promise of potential and the provision of power we have been given as followers of Jesus Christ, many believers are functioning in their work without knowledge of their potential or the power that's available to them. They are operating in their own power or on what I call "cruise control." While there may be those who think that some movement is better than no movement, the truth of the matter is that if we are to reach the potential Christ promises in John the 14th chapter, minimum performance, of our own devices, is not acceptable.

For example, while an automobile is able to reach speeds in excess of 100 m.p.h., we typically do not utilize the full power of the car's engine. The same is true for many in the church. Many of us have yet to discover the full power available to us through Jesus Christ. We are operating on cruise control.

One of the dangers of operating in our own power, or on cruise, is that it causes us to become less attentive. As is the case when a driver sets his cruise control in his car, drivers have the tendency to become listless. In the spiritual sense, when you're not operating in the fullness of Christ's power, but in your own limited power, you've predetermined your speed or progression in the Lord's work. You are timing your own destiny. As a fully-developing follower of Christ, we cannot be as productive as God desires when we are on cruise control, when we've already decided not to use the power that's available to us. Jesus was not totally predictable in His ministry nor does He expect us to be in ours. As is the case with any driver, you eventually reach a point when we no longer desire to operate on cruise - we may need to pass a slowing motorist, a police car may appear, or we may find ourselves drifting off to sleep. Whatever the problem, we dis-engage the cruise control when something unexpected hap-pens. Much is the case in the life of the cruising Christian. Those unexpected events cause us to get off of cruise. Crisis gets our attention and we suddenly want a closer walk with God. We want to really hear from Him. Or if we need to pass, or desire to get ahead, then we disengage cruise because of that new job we want. Once we get through our crises, our tendency is to return to cruise.

We are on cruise when we depend on our own ability. We know how to perform the functions of the church - how to direct the choir, how to arrange the chairs, how to count the money, when to raise our hands, and when to say amen - but the true work of the church cannot be accomplished without power from the Holy Spirit. We cannot be true Christians without the aid of the Holy Spirit.

As we begin to recognize the Holy Spirit and the work He desires to do through us, we can operate in the power that Christ gave to us to become catalysts for change in our environments. If we are truly to move to the next level, we need to operate in the power of the Holy Spirit in order to bring

> *We cannot be true Christians without the aid of the Holy Spirit.*

about change and transformation in our lives and in the lives of those who are without Christ. We have been endowed with a power such that we can affect our surroundings and the people in them for the better. It was never Jesus' intention for believers to function on anything less than the fullness of power He provided. We were called to make a difference. Unfortunately, it is not uncommon to hear fellow brothers and sisters in Christ complaining about the ill condition of others.

From the evil state of their co-workers to the rebellious nature of their children, people are frustrated with the state of their environments. If we are to go to the next level, we would stop condemning others and actively seek the power Christ provides to bring about change and transformation. Our surroundings should be changing for the better because of the power within us. It is then that we will begin to experience greater degrees of greatness, or the "greater works," in our ministries. We need to evaluate our ministries and the impact we are having on the lives of those around us.

Where Does God Want Me To Be?

In order to achieve next level power, you must have faith. Anyone who has faith in Jesus Christ, in who He is as the Son of God must also have faith in what He did as well as what He said during his ministry on earth. This faith has the potential to move mountains. We must move beyond thinking of the Bible and its recordings of

Believers are to experience greater degrees of greatness, or the "greater works," in their ministries.

Jesus merely as a history lesson. Because it tells believers of Christ and his works of power, and subsequently promises the same and even greater works by His disciples, we should be making history today. By having faith in Jesus Christ, what seems impossible becomes possible. We must have faith in the work of Christ before the cross, on the cross and after the cross.

Faith must be coupled with prayer. Jesus was a man of prayer. He constantly sought the Father for direction. As a result of His constant praying, He received more power. The believer's availability of power can be measured by how much time they are willing to spend with God. In our consistent praying, we can ask for power. Prayer provides the stage whereby the believer may make a request of God. As we seek to become a fully-developing follower of Jesus Christ, our requests should extend beyond physical things. We commonly ask God for health, wealth, employment and those things we need to function in our daily lives. But how many of us have asked God for more power in our lives to live as transformed men and women? How many of us have asked for more power, so much so, that we draw those around us who are hurting and in need of a personal relationship with Christ? We must pray for power.

> *We must have faith in the work of Christ before the cross, on the cross and after the cross.*

Obedience is imperative in the life of the believer. As we seek to do the work of God in the power He provides, we must

44

follow the guidance of the Holy Spirit. Our obedience is two-fold. Not only is the believer to read and obey the Word of God, but also the voice of the Holy Spirit. When we are obedient, Jesus mainifests Himself to us in power.

And finally, if we are to achieve next level power, faith, prayer and obedience are necessities. We have been given the Holy Spirit, the power of God, to accomplish the work He has for us. God wants us to experience the privilege of knowing Him in the work He has for us.

> *Not only is the believer to read and obey the Word of God, but also the voice of the Holy Spirit.*

Study Guide: Moving To Next Level Power

1. Next level power is available to _____ believer.

2. We were never intended to operate in the body of Christ on anything _____ than the power He provides in the person of the Holy Spirit.

3. We _____ be true Christians without the aid of the Holy Spirit.

4. Believers are to experience _____ degrees of greatness, or the "greater works," in their ministries.

5. We must have _____ in the work of Christ before the cross, on the cross and after the cross.

6. How does the Lord want you to positively affect your environment through next level power?

7. Not only is the believer to read and obey the Word of God, but also the _____ of the Holy Spirit.

8. What do the following scriptures have to say about power?

    Ephesians 1:18-19

    Ephesians 3:7

    Colossians 1:29

9. Scripture Memory: Ephesians 6:10

4

Next Level Peace

Philippians 4:4-9 NIV

4 Rejoice in the Lord always. I will say it again: Rejoice!

5 Let your gentleness be evident to all. The Lord is near.

6 Do not be anxious about anything, but in everything, by prayer and petition, with thanksgiving, present your requests to God.

7 And the peace of God, which transcends all understanding, will guard your hearts and your minds in Christ Jesus.

8 Finally, brothers, whatever is true, whatever is noble, whatever is right, whatever is pure, whatever is lovely, whatever is admirable - if anything is excellent or praiseworthy - think about such things.

9 Whatever you have learned or received or heard from me, or seen in me - put it into practice. And the God of peace will be with you.

In spite of America being the most advanced and economically strong country in the world, with its fortune 500 companies, 401k's, profit sharing, nice offices, cars, homes, clothes and its many other luxuries, the thing that most Americans lack is inner peace.

Because of our life experiences, many believers have become insecure, pessimistic and angry. This is not the proper mindset of a Christian in light of the fact that Jesus came that we might have life and have it to the full, or more abundantly (John 10:10 NIV). In our walk with Christ, we have discovered that Christianity does not offer us immunity from problems, pain or persecution. Robert McGee notes in his book, *Search For Significance* that "As Christians, our fulfillment in life depends not on our skills to avoid life's problems, but on our ability to apply God's specific solutions to those problems."[1] In spite of any problem we may face, we must be assured that the peace of God, next level peace, is available to us.

What Is Next Level Peace?

Next level peace is a powerful, penetrating, tranquil, restful state that can be experienced by a believer who is assured of their salvation, and content with God's care in the face of trouble. It is a condition that cannot be produced by man and a state that cannot be fully understood by us.

What Must Be Considered?

There are several reasons why many of us do not have next level peace. I will focus on the predominant reasons I believe are common in most of our lives. I will use the acronym **P-E-A-C-E** to give 5 reasons why many people do not have next level peace in their lives today.

P

As much as we love our parents, we have to admit that the reason why many of us do not have peace is because of our parental upbringing. The reason many of us are like we are today is because of what happened in our homes as children. We may not have felt loved, respected or were exposed to abuse in some form. More often than not, we are the products of our parents.

E

The second reason we do not have peace is because of our environment. More specifically, our past or present environment could be robbing us of the peace God desires for us. Maybe there were not individuals who served as examples of peace for us or the conditions of our environment did not promote peace. In fact, our surroundings may have influenced or is influencing our level of peace.

A

The third cause for our lack of peace is that many of us have a problem with the authority figures in our lives. We don't like anyone telling us what to do. We feel as if our authority figures are always picking on us or they think they are better than us. We don't like to be around them. We dislike being subject to them and this prevents us from being content. We fail to have peace because we do not have the proper respect for authority.

C

The fourth reason we don't have peace is because of a past or present crisis. In fact, if we really had to testify, some of us would have to say our whole lives have been one big crisis after another. We get the car fixed and then the hot water heater goes bad. We get the house painted and then the roof begins to leak. You get over the flu only to find out that you have diabetes. Or you get a new job and then the company has layoffs. Crisis seems to be ongoing in our lives. Thus, we are never free from it long enough to have peace.

E

The fifth reason we fail to have peace is our emotions. We are suffering from some form of emotional stress as a result of a bad relationship or experience. We put our trust in someone or something and they betrayed that trust. We are carrying the baggage from those experiences and consequently cannot enjoy next level peace.

Where Does God Want Me To Be?

We already have peace with God because we are saved. That means the wrath of God is not directed at us. We are not headed to condemnation. We are not headed to damnation. We are not headed to hell. But, what we need is the peace of God. The Hebrew word for peace is *shâlôm* which also applies to health, soundness, prosperity and well-being. We need to move to that next level of peace in our lives. The psalmist gives further insight into this truth, *"Great peace have they who love your law, and nothing can make them stumble" (Psalm 119:165 NIV).*

Great peace or next level peace, is the direct result of

loving God's Word. Believers cannot walk in the peace of God apart from His Word. In other words, we may be experiencing peace in our homes but not on our jobs. We have peace in some areas of our lives but not every area. Many of God's children have been living on a "piece-meal peace" instead of the "great peace" spoken of by the psalmist. Next level peace is a peace that encompasses all of our lives. God's Word will relieve and remedy our lack of peace. Paul gives us the pathway to great peace when he wrote to the church at Philippi. He was not writing without personal knowledge of the next level peace

> *Many of God's children have been living on a "piece-meal peace" instead of the "great peace" spoken of by the psalmist.*

God provides. In fact, when he wrote the letter to the church at Philippi, he was imprisoned. No other person could share the pathway to peace like the Apostle Paul. In spite of his imprisonment, he wrote a letter of encouragement. He instructs those at the church of Philippi, as well as present-day believers, to praise the Lord. He writes, *"Rejoice in the Lord always. I will say it again: Rejoice!" (Philippians 4:4 NIV).*

Paul demonstrates the necessity to praise the Lord, in spite of our circumstances. He rejoiced in the Lord in spite of his imprisonment and we are to do the same in spite of the prisons in which we may be trapped. Whether it be in the area of our finances, relationships, sickness, or otherwise, we must look for reasons to praise the Lord. The psalmist further declares, *"I will extol the Lord at all times; his praise will always be on my lips" (Psalm 34:1 NIV)*.

Next level peace is patient. As we praise the Lord in our trials, we are to be patient. Paul writes in his letter to the church, *"Let your gentleness be evident to all. The Lord is near" (Philippians 4:5 NIV)*.

The Greek word for moderation is *epieikes* which means "mild, gentle or patient." Paul is telling us that as we deal with others, we must practice patience. When we deal with people, they should recognize our ability to be fair, considerate and equitable. They should also see our willingness to restrain from judgmental or punitive behavior. Our reason for practicing patience as noted by Paul in scripture is because, "The Lord is near." Paul could have meant that Christ's second coming is going to be in the near future or that the Lord is always near to us in any of our circumstances. In either instance, we should not be alarmed. Next level peace becomes possible when we are mindful of God's abiding presence.

The practice of patience is two-fold. While we must practice patience with others, we must also be patient with God. The Greek word for peace is *eirene* which describes "harmonious relationships between men, nations, between God and man, a freedom from, and a sense of contentment." We are never to forget the Lord's closeness to us even in the midst of pain, problems and persecution. As we practice patience, in dealing with our difficulties and in faithfully waiting on God's deliverance, we are learning to trust God. We are demonstrating that we trust Him to deliver us from any predicament.

> *While we must practice patience with others, we must also be patient with God.*

Next level peace prays thankfully. We must also learn to pray thankfully. Paul writes, *"Don't be anxious about anything, but in everything, by prayer and petition, with thanksgiving, present your requests to God" (Philippians 4:6 NIV).*

The word "anxious" means to be troubled with care. In doing so, we are to thank God in advance for His answer. We often seek peace in many ways. We may try exercising or maintaining a proper diet. While these practices may prove beneficial to our physical welfare, true peace is achieved through prayer. There can be no peace without prayer. If we are to know the next level peace God has for us, we must pray with the assurance of God's commitment to us and our well-being.

Next level peace prays positively. Just because you feel imprisoned in various areas of your life doesn't mean that you have to pray a "prison-prayer." Believers should not approach prayer as if

There can be no peace without prayer.

life is all over. We must be assured of God's desire for our betterment and His ability to deliver us from any situation.

Next level peace prays persistently. We must also be persistent in prayer. Not because God is hard of hearing, but because we must consistently exercise prayer as the remedy to our problems. The fulfillment of next level peace is the result of continually seeking God.

Next level peace prays persuasively. Believers must pray persuasively. By this, I am not suggesting that we need to try and persuade God, for He knows us and our hearts better than we do. But next level peace is achieved when we are fully persuaded of God's commitment to us. Our individual persuasion in God's ability to answer our request must be evident in our prayers.

Next level peace prays purposefully. Believers must be

intent in their request. If you want deliverance, at some point in your prayer shouldn't you ask for it? We can be specific in our requests. Scripture reports that when we have the peace of God, it will guard our hearts and minds. *"And the peace of God which transcends all understanding, will guard your hearts and your minds in Christ Jesus" (Philippians 4:7 NIV).*

Our individual persuasion in God's ability to answer our request must be evident in our prayers.

In other words, the purpose of peace is to keep us in a restful and tranquil state. Next level peace will form a protective barrier around our hearts and minds so that when we want to flee from the turmoil going on around us, it will be a barrier around us enabling us to remain and wait on the deliverance of God. In fact, through next level peace, we can experience God's deliverance in the midst of our turmoil! And while the enemy may attempt to rob us of our assurance in the security of Christ, next level peace, brought about by the constant meditation on God's Word, will inhibit the attack launched against us, and cause it to be ineffective. Thus, the peace of God will guard us in all our ways.

Study Guide: Moving To Next Level Peace

1. We fail to have peace because of:

   a._____

   b._____

   c._____

   d._____

   e._____

2. Many of God's children have been living on a _____ instead of the "great peace" spoken of by the psalmist.

3. While we must practice patience with others, we must also be patient with _____.

4. There can be no peace without _____.

5. The extent of our _____ in God's ability to answer our request must be evident in our prayers.

6. Next level peace is _____.

7. Next level peace prays:

      a. _____

      b. _____

      c. _____

      d. _____

8. What do the following scripture verses share about next level peace?

    Romans 16:20

    2 Corinthians 13:11

    2 Thessalonians 3:16

9. Scripture Memory: Hebrews 13:20-21

5
Next Level Corporate Peace

Colossians 3:15 NIV

15 Let the peace of Christ rule in your hearts, since as members of one body you were called to peace. And be thankful.

One way to describe the local church is to use the word "community." This word depicts the transparent interaction, the open fellowship and genuine relationship that bind people of different backgrounds together. In every local faith community, there are so many differences among members: education, skills, experiences, marital status, socio-economic status, spiritual gifting, needs, desires, maturity levels, world views and much more. Only "community" can bring about oneness and cohesion among these differences.

What Is Next Level Corporate Peace?

Next level corporate peace is the state achieved by a congregation wherein talking, listening, caring, knowing, serving and giving are priorities exercised in order to accomplish the mission given and guided by God.

What Must Be Considered?

When community exists within a local congregation, the body of Christ thrives. Programs, activities, buildings, events or crowds do not bind people together. These things do not bring life and health to a congregation. A congregation should be a living, functioning community. The term "master-planned" is used to attract new homebuyers to a new subdivision. This term implies that everything has been planned and provided for new homeowners including schools and parks. And, one of the features of this type of development is that it promotes peace and tranquility.

The local church is a "Master-planned" community. It has been planned by the Lord Jesus Christ to be a community of oneness, identifying with Him and drawing the unsaved, the untaught and the unchurched to Him. In order for this to happen within a local church, there must be peace. The Hebrew word for peace is *shalom* which means, "health, soundness, prosperity, and well-being." The Greek word for peace is *eirene*. It describes harmonious relationships between men, between nations, between God and man, freedom from outside intrusion, and a sense of contentment.

So important was the concept of peace that when Jesus met with the Apostles after His resurrection, John 20:19 NIV records His first words to them as, *"Peace be with you."* The Apostle Paul championed this Jewish idea of peace often in his letters, *"Grace to you and peace from God our Father, and the Lord Jesus Christ" (Romans 1:7 NIV),* and, *"...and the God of peace shall be with you" (Philippians 4:9 NIV).* *"Peace be to the brethren, and love with faith, from God the Father and the Lord Jesus Christ" (Ephesians 6:23 NIV)* and, *"And be at peace among yourselves"* (*1 Thessalonians 5:13 NIV*). *"Let the peace of Christ rule in your hearts, since as members of one body you were called to peace. And be thankful"* (*Colossians 3:15 NIV*).

Where Does God Want Me To Be?

Paul taught that peace should characterize the community of believers. He puts forth that peace be the criterion for recognizing God in the life of the individual as well as the community of believers. Therefore, when people come to the campus of the local church, they should sense the manifestation of peace in the community. They should be able to smell it, see it, taste it, hear it and feel it!

In the world, there is plenty of discord, conflict, fighting, competition, rivalry, war, and strife. There's plenty of that in politics, academia, corporate america, family and among neighbors. The last thing that the local church needs is for lost or hurting people to turn to or stumble upon the campus of the church for salvation, deliverance or answers to their chaos and find people fussing and fighting.

> *When people come to the campus of the local church, they should sense the manifestation of peace in the community.*

Paul presents a practical process for peace in the church community. *"Put to death, therefore, whatever belongs to your earthly nature: sexual immorality, impurity, lust, evil desires and greed, which is idolatry," (Colossians 3:5 NIV).* Even though a person is "saved" they will still have sinful inclinations and tendencies. By and large, there is something that is hidden and just waiting to come out of each of us at any moment. It just needs the right stimuli. In verses 8 and 9, Paul says, *"rid yourselves of all such things as these: anger, rage, malice, slander, and filthy language from your lips since you have taken off your old self with its practices."*

Peace is dependent upon us taking off some stuff! We cannot have peace in the local church when people live, think and behave in opposition to God's Word. Peace exists when members of the church community live in fellowship with God, which requires the getting rid of the old-world, fleshly, self-centered nature. The old self deters peace and incurs the wrath of God. So, put it off! Paul alludes to clothing to make his point. Clothes should be taken off for the

> *We cannot have peace in the local church when people live, think and behave in opposition to God's Word.*

following reasons: when they don't match, when they don't fit, when they are soiled or dirty, when they are not designed for you, or when they don't suit the occasion. What Paul would say to us today is, "Anger doesn't match your new nature. Rage doesn't fit your new identity in the Lord. Malice is a dirty stain on your heart. Slander is not designed for God's children. Filthy language is never proper for the believer. Take it off!"

Peace in relationships and interaction among members requires us not just to put off some things but also to put on some things. Paul suggests that the believer put on or be arrayed in a character, personality, temperament or moral fiber that resembles Christ. The new man is to be like Christ. *"Therefore as God's chosen people holy and dearly loved, clothe yourselves with compassion, kindness, humility, gentleness and patience" (Colossians 3:12 NIV).* Each of the qualities Paul mentions has to do with personal relationships that help believers to fellowship and interact with each other. When there is compassion, kindness, humility, gentleness and patience operating in relationships, there will be peace, power and productivity in the church. These qualities have to be put on by individual believers. These qualities cannot be put on an individual. The believer has to do this personally in order to be at peace. Ephesians 4:24 NIV reads, *"put on the new self created to be like god in true righteousness and holiness."*

Our new man is like a new garment that may take some time to fit comfortably after it is worn several times, it becomes comfortable. We can then begin to demonstrate a new attitude. "New man" means new attitude! God's Word reports, *"if anyone is in Christ, he is a new creation, the old has gone, the new has come"* *(2 Corinthians 5:17 NIV).*

Believers in the church also need to put up with one another. *"Bear with each other and forgive whatever grievances you may have against one another. Forgive as the Lord forgave you" (Colossians 3:13 NIV).* For peace to be evident, members of the local church have to put up with each other. This is known as forbearance which means to suffer or endure with others. Since people are not perfect, we have to exercise forbearance. Since people are on different levels of spiritual maturity, there has to be forbearance. Since Satan is still busy within our congregations, there has to be forbearance. In other words, we have to tolerate each other. Ideally, there should be a "zero tolerance policy" against intolerance in the church. Intolerance is the attitude and behavior that does not accept or accommodate people who are different or who have made mistakes. Intolerance produces bitterness, anger, revenge, division, selfishness, hatred, grudges, fighting, and a mean spirit. Paul teaches that we have to forgive. We've got to forgive just as Christ forgives us. Peace calls for a pardoning spirit among believers. This can only be done when love is active. *"Love covers a multitude of sins"* *(1 Peter 4:8 NIV).* Love is the perfect fulfillment of what God expects of us in our relationships. Love must be in every person and ministry of the church.

> *There should be a "zero tolerance policy" again intolerance in the church.*

Peace is a personal responsibility before it becomes a corporate responsibility. When, peace is recognized as a personal responsibility, it can be realized within the relationships in the body. The individual and the corporate body must allow peace to operate. *"Let the peace of God rule in your hearts" (Colossians 3:15).* The word Paul uses for rule means, "umpire" in the Greek language. We know that an umpire in sports decides, determines, or directs circumstances in games with the overriding objective of keeping order and peace. Therefore, peace has to rule in our hearts. It has to umpire the situations, circumstances and the interaction between members in the church. Once a violation of the rules occurs, the umpire notifies the players and the spectators of the violation by blowing a whistle. Next level peace occurs in the local church when members allow peace to umpire their thoughts, intentions, communication, facial expressions, mannerisms, and the like. Members should "blow the whistle" on themselves first, in order to keep order and peace. Then members should "blow the whistle" on other members when the things they should have put off attempt to display themselves. Remember what Jesus taught, *"Blessed are the peacemakers for they will be called sons of God" (Matthew 5:9 NIV).* The inner man must control the behavior and attitude of the believer not life's circumstances. The

Next level peace occurs in the local church when members allow peace to umpire their thoughts, intentions, communication, facial expressions, mannerisms, and the like.

believer is called to rejoice, be glad and praise the Lord in all circumstances. The believer is called to peace.

Study Guide: Moving To Next Level Corporate Peace

1. The Greek word for peace, eirene, describes harmonious
   _____ between men, between nations, between
   God and man, freedom from outside intrusion and a sense
   of contentment.

2. When people come to the campus of the local church,
   they should sense the manifestation of _____.

3. We cannot have peace in the local church when people
   live, think and behave in opposition to God's
   _____.

4. There should be a "zero tolerance policy" against
   _____.

5. Next level peace occurs in the local church when members allow peace to _____ their thoughts, intentions, communication, facial expressions, mannerisms
   and the like.

6. Community is talking, listening, caring, knowing, serving, giving, in essence _____.

7. A _____ should be a living, functioning community.

8. Peace is dependent upon us taking _____ some stuff.

9. Peace in relationships and interaction among members requires us not just to put off but also to put _____.

10. Believers in the church also need to put _____ with one another.

11. Peace is a _____ responsibility before it becomes a corporate responsibility.

12. What do the following verses share about next level peace?
    John 14:27

Psalm 34:14

Romans 14:19

13. Scripture Memory: John 14:27

6

Next Level Praise

Hebrews 13:15 NIV

15 Through Jesus, therefore, let us continually offer God a sacrifice of praise - the fruit of lips that confess his name.

Many believers do not know how to properly offer praise to God. This is an area of weakness in many of our Christian lives. Because of our lack of understanding, the praise we give to God lacks vitality, skill, volume, power, purpose, consistency, intensity and thought. Unfortunately, our praise to God is something we don't try to improve upon or sharpen. We do other things with intensity, but when it comes to praise, often times, it's weak.

What Is Next Level Praise?

Next level praise is the expression of admonition and approval of the blessings of God that may be inconvenient to the worshipper, but is precious and done with a willing heart.

What Must Be Considered?

In the Old Testament, the Hebraic people were required to bring an offering to worship. They could not go to the temple without an offering that was given to God in the form of a sacrifice.

There were burnt offerings. Worshippers brought bulls, sheep or goats to be offered to God. And if you were poor, you were not exempt. You could get a turtledove or a pigeon. There was the meal offering or the grain offering. People brought offerings of flour or meal from their harvest and it was mixed with oil or frankincense and sometimes they would make unleavened cakes with the best flour and season it with salt.

There was the peace offering. These offerings were done to express gratitude to God and fellowship with Him. They were mainly associated with the celebrations of Jewish life. In this offering, they were to bring an unblemished animal to be sacrificed to the Lord.

There was the sin offering. In this offering an animal sacrifice was made to atone for sins. An offering was made on behalf of the mistakes that one would make in life, for the rash acts committed.

There was the the trespass offering. This was an animal sacrifice for unintentional sins. This offering expressed that you wanted to right your sins, that you wanted to get your life straight with God. Many times the individual had to pay some form of restitution for the acts they had done.

Like the sacrifices offered in the Old Testament, a sacrifice is an offering or the giving up of something precious and of value. It was an inconvenient act, but it was done with a willing heart. The requirement is still the same today. Our sacrifices to God are not to be rendered only when it is convenient for us. In fact, the level of our commitment may quite honestly be determined by whether or not we can make a sacrifice to God when it is not convenient. A sacrifice can only be classified as a sacrifice when it costs us something in order to give it whether it be our time, money or effort. In spite of it's inconvenience it must be done with a willing heart.

The writer of Hebrews teaches us that the old sacrificial system has passed away and the new covenant relationship with God is now established through Jesus Christ. He entered into Heaven and appears before God for us. Our whole faith system is now based upon Jesus Christ. His death was a one-time sacrifice, a one-time offering. God's Word reads, *"Unlike the other high priests, he does not need to offer sacrifices day after day, first for his own sins, and then for the sins of the people. He sacrificed for their sins once for all when he offered himself"* (Hebrews 7:27 NIV). And, *"For Christ did not enter a man-made sanctuary that was only a copy of the true one; he entered heaven itself, not to appear for us in God's presence. Nor did he enter heaven to offer himself again and again, the way the high priest enters the Most Holy Place every year with blood that is not his own. Then Christ would have had to suffer many times since the creation of the world. But now he has appeared once for all at the end of the ages to do away with sin by the sacrifice of himself. Just as man is destined to die once, and after that to face judgment, so Christ was sacrificed once to take away the sins of many people; and he will appear a second time, not to bear sin, but to bring salvation to those who are waiting for him" (Hebrews 9:24-28 NIV).* Under the new covenant, God's people are placed in a new position with a new practice. We are now priests.

Where Does God Want Me To Be?

Next level praise is not fixed to a special circumstance or season. Next level praise is continuous and is not confined to a specific time or place. Some believers offer God seasonal praise and thanksgiving. They offer praise to the Lord on specific occasions or only under certain circumstances. They wait until special events such as choir concerts or Thanksgiving Day worship service to offer praise to God. Their emotions must be properly stimulated in order for them to participate in praise. Or Sunday morning worship service is the only place or time when they can

Next level praise is continuous!

get in the spirit of praise. Praise should not be limited to the confines of the church. Believers should possess a praise that can be expressed anywhere. God is worthy of our praise at all times even in the absence of special events or extraordinary blessings we may experience. *"I will extol the LORD at all times; his praise will always be on my lips" (Psalm 34:1 NIV).*

Next level praise is not solely established for a special group. All believers are to praise the Lord. In our everyday lives, we have the opportunity to choose to praise the Lord. Praise is a choice. We can choose to focus on the negatives or positives in our lives.

Next level praise is not relegated to specific circumstances. It is not being blind to the trying occurrences we experience, but being determined in our wills not to focus on or allow those negative or unpleasant occurrences to rule our attitudes or thankfulness to God. It is choosing to express to Him our adoration for His character and who He is, in spite of what we may be experiencing.

Next level praise is the praise that comes from our lips. It is the audible expression of the inward and invisible workings of God, which produce an outward, identifiable evidence of thankfulness. It is a part of the believer's testimony. We witness to the goodness and power of God when we verbally praise Him. Next level praise is verbal. Praise is not praise

until it is heard. The psalmist wrote, *"Praise our God, O peoples, let the sound of his praise be heard" (Psalm 66:8 NIV).*
He further tells us to *"Shout for joy to the Lord, all the earth. Worship the Lord with gladness; come before him with joyful songs. Know that the Lord is God. It is*

Next level praise is verbal.

he who made us, and we are him; we are his people, the sheep of his pasture. Enter his gates with thanksgiving and his courts with praise; give thanks to him and praise his name. For the Lord is good and his love endures forever; his faithfulness continues through all generations" (Psalm 100 NIV).

Next level praise is offered through Christ, with Christ on the mind and in the heart of the believer. This sacrifice is effective because of the name in which the praise is offered - Jesus Christ. Offering praise in His name speaks of His authority, character, rank, majesty power and excellence. *"Therefore God exalted him to the highest place and gave him the name that is above every name, that at the*

Next level praise is effectual.

name of Jesus every knee should bow, in heaven and on earth and under the earth" (Philippians 2:9-10 NIV). Praise pleases God.

Study Guide: Moving To Next Level Praise

1. Next level praise is _____!

2. Next level praise is not solely established for a

   _____.

3. Next level praise is not relegated to _____.

4. Next level praise is offered through _____, with
   Christ on the mind and heart of the believer.

5. The Jews of the Old Testament were always required to
   bring some type of sacrifice when they worshipped God.
   A sacrifice was an offering or giving up of something
   precious and of value. The act was inconvenient, but
   done with a _____ heart.

6. In the Old Testament, there were different types of sacrifices:

   a. _____

   b. _____

c. _____

d. _____

7. Next level praise is _____.

8. Next level praise is _____.

9. What do the following scriptures share about next level praise?

    Psalm 69:30-31

    Psalm 107:21-22

    Psalm 116:17

10. Scripture Memory: Psalm 118:19

7

Next Level Participation

Romans 12:1-8 NIV

1 Therefore, I urge you, brothers, in view of God's mercy, to offer your bodies as living sacrifices, holy and pleasing to God--this is your spiritual act of worship.

2 Do not conform any longer to the pattern of this world, but be transformed by the renewing of your mind. Then you will be able to test and approve what God's will is--his good, pleasing and perfect will.

3 For by the grace given me I say to every one of you: Do not think of yourself more highly than you ought, but rather think of yourself with sober judgment, in accordance with the measure of faith God has given you.

4 Just as each of us has one body with many members, and these members do not all have the same function,

5 so in Christ we who are many form one body, and each member belongs to all the others.

6 We have different gifts, according to the grace given us. If a man's gift is prophesying, let him use it in proportion to his faith.

7 If it is serving, let him serve; if it is teaching, let him teach;

8 if it is encouraging, let him encourage; if it is contributing to the needs of others, let him give generously; if it is leadership, let him govern diligently; if it is showing mercy, let him do it cheerfully.

83

The United States of American can presently brag about something that the 21st century church cannot - a lowered unemployment rate. We have as many people who've joined the local church but are not employed in its ministries. Most churches could hang a "Help Wanted" sign in the window every Sunday of the year.

Most churches face the fact that far too many members are uninvolved, unknown or unseen until Sunday morning worship. In this present church culture of consumerism, people are riding the pews without shame. These people are spectators rather than participants in the work of the church.

As any pastor or church leader will attest, participation of their members is essential to the growth of their ministry. As Christ fulfilled His earthly ministry, He enlisted selected men and women to participate in the plan of redemption He would later secure for mankind through his life, death and resurrection.

From the wedding servants who filled the water pots with water which subsequently was turned into wine, to Simon of Cyrene's help in carrying the cross to Calvary, the participation from these, as well as others, was essential. Likewise, present-day believers are called to participate in the work of the church.

What Is Next Level Participation?

Next level participation is knowing and sharing in the manifestation of the vision of your church while perceiving that work as your task and God-given privilege.

What Must Be Considered?

We all are at some level of participation in ministry. As a fully-developing follower of Christ, you must participate in the work of the ministry at your local church. You should be involved so that the vision of your church can become a reality. The problem is not so much where you presently are, but not knowing and staying there.

The problem is not so much where you presently are but not knowing where you are and staying where you are.

There are six levels of participation that I will discuss:

- ◆Committed Compliance,
- ◆Genuine Compliance,
- ◆Formal Compliance,
- ◆Grudging Compliance,
- ◆Non-Compliance,
- ◆and Apathy.[1]

Committed Compliance

As a participant in ministry, you are committed and want the vision and are doing only what it takes to bring it to fruition.

Genuine Compliance

As a participant in ministry, you want the vision, but will only do so much to help bring it to pass.

Formal Compliance

As a participant in ministry, you work toward the fulfillment of the vision by doing what is expected and nothing more.

Grudging Compliance

As a participant in ministry, you do just enough, but complain and execute your task in a grudging manner.

Non-Compliance

As a participant in ministry, you see the needs that exist in the ministry and just refuse to participate.

Apathy

As a participant in ministry, you are neither for nor against the work of the church and you invest no interest, passion or money.

A lack of participation in the ministries of the church produces ineffective programs. When individuals do not share their gifts within the body of Christ, the church suffers. Spiritual gifts are given for the strengthening of the church. *"Now to each one the manifestation of the Spirit is given for the common good" (1 Corinthians 12:7).* Christ never intended the work of ministry to be the task of one or two people, but that the body of believers share in the work. It takes the combined efforts of believers to produce the results God desires.

> *It takes the combined efforts of believers to produce the results God desires.*

If people do not participate in the work of the ministry, their lack of participation places a great burden on a few who are willing to participate. After an extended period of time, when a few people have been doing the work of several people, burnout is inevitable.

The Spirit of God has given each of us one or more spiritual gifts. *"To one there is given through the Spirit the message of wisdom, to another the message of knowledge by means of the same Spirit, to another faith by the same Spirit, to another gifts of healing by that one Spirit, to another miraculous powers, to another prophecy, to another distin-*

87

guishing between spirits, to another speaking in different kinds of tongues, and to still another the interpretation of tongues. All these are the work of one and the same Spirit, and he gives them to each one, just as he determines" (1 Corinthians 12:8-11 NIV). It is the combining of those gifts that allow the church to be fruitful in its work. Without adequate participation in the work of the ministry, something will always go lacking.

> *Without adequate participation in the work of the ministry, something will always go lacking.*

When the unemployed were studied in America, these facts will most typically be found:

- ◆Some people don't want to work;
- ◆Some people choose not to work;
- ◆Some can't work due to sickness or disability;
- ◆Some enter the workforce only in times of personal crisis; and
- ◆Some are not adequately trained.

The unemployed of the church resemble those in secular society.

We must begin to recognize that God has provided the church with sufficient resources to carry out its mission. Each parishioner is present in the congregation for a reason. The participation and involvement of every member can meet the needs of the ministry. While everyone's contribution will not be the same, it is the sum of every contribution that enables the church to meet its desired end.

Where Does God Want Me To Be?

Next level participation is the result of understanding our purpose. You may ask yourself, "Why participate?" Paul urges us in Romans 12:1 to move to a higher level of participation. The attention in verse one is on the individual. *"Therefore, I urge you, brothers, in view of God's mercy, to offer your bodies as living sacrifices, holy and pleasing to God - this is your spiritual act of worship" (Romans 12:1 NIV).*

The premise for participation is "in view of God's mercy." Each believer should be motivated to apply or sign up for ministry in the local church because of God's great compassion. There should be zero unemployment because none of us received from God what we deserved. *"For the wages of sin is death, but the gift of God is eternal life in Christ Jesus our Lord" (Romans 6:23 NIV).*

God has a purpose for every individual that is saved. Purpose is discovered when one places his body sacrifically at God's disposal. The word "offer" in the Greek language means to place a person or thing at another's disposal. Paul tells us that our participation, the yielding of our bodies, is our spiritual act of worship. We are to be God's instruments through whom He accomplishes His work. This requires an active participation of the spirit, soul and body of the believer. It simply is not possible without our continuous yielding to the will of God in our lives. We are told in 1 Corinthians 6:19-20 that we are not our own, but we are bought with a price.

> *Believers must understand that we are to submit our physical bodies and its use to the will of God.*

If we are going to achieve next level participation, we must accept the truth that the purpose of the believer's body is to be the temple of the Holy Spirit. Believers must understand that we are to submit our physical bodies and its use to the will of God.

Next level participation requires us to consecrate and dedicate our minds to God's transforming Word through study and meditation. Once we become committed in our roles within the body of Christ, we then may be of benefit to our brothers and sisters as God designed through participation and the rendering of service to and for one another. Next level participation not only understands that this is our purpose, but it also accepts this as our privilege. We are to follow the example modeled by Christ who did not come to be served but to serve. We are told in Philippians 2:6-8 NIV, *"Who, being in very nature God, did not consider equality with God something to be grasped, but made himself nothing, taking the very nature of a servant, being made in human likeness. And being found in appearance as a man, he humbled himself and became obedient to death - even death on a cross!"* As a result of our next level participation, we become more Christ-like.

The next level participant has a proper perspective. We need to evaluate our mindsets regarding the work of the church. The proper perspective is necessary for increasing levels of participation - a proper perspective of oneself, other members, and the importance of the church. The Word of God says, *"For by the grace given me I say to every one of you: Do not think of yourself more highly than you ought, but rather think of yourself with sober judgment, in accordance with the measure of faith God has given you. Just as each of us has one body with many members, and these members do not all have the same function, so in Christ we who are many*

> *The proper perspective is necessary for increasing levels of participation - a proper perspective of oneself, other members, and the importance of the church.*

form one body, and each member belongs to all the others"
(Romans 12:3-5 NIV).

Paul encourages us to have a proper perspective. It is a must with today's highly educated and technically-skilled membership. Some of these are not participating because they see involvement in the work of the church as an inferior work. Paul would say to them, "Do not think of yourself more highly than you ought." You have something to offer!

Another concern in the local church has to be for the multiple job holders. These are the over-employed who are holding so many positions that they intentionally or unintentionally make others feel that there are no openings. Paul would say again, "Do not think of yourself more highly than you ought." Take off some of those hats you're wearing. The church is a body and everybody is needed. To move to the next level in our participation we need to assess our personal potential, accept God's purpose and gifting and assume the personal responsibility for making a noticeable difference. Believers should view their gifts and abilities to serve in the church as privileges. Paul knew that the local church is only as strong as the total use of the individual spiritual gifts of its members. That is why he encourages every member to serve.

God gave believers spiritual gifts for the perfecting of the body of Christ. Our gifts were intended to be shared and utilized in the work and edification of believers. God has granted us the opportunity to serve in the work of His church. *"Each one should use whatever gift he has received to serve others, faithfully administering God's grace in its various forms" (1 Peter 4:10 NIV)* and, *"We have different gifts, according to the grace given us. If a man's gift is*

> *Believers should view their gifts and abilities to serve in the church as privileges.*

prophesying, let him use it in proportion to his faith. If it is serving, let him serve; if it is teaching, let him teach; if it is encouraging, let him encourage; if it is contributing to the needs of others, let him give generously; if it is leadership, let him govern diligently; if it is showing mercy, let him do it cheerfully" (Romans 12:6-8 NIV). I like this translation because of its permission-emphasis "let him." The tension is now on the church and its leaders to encourage service from every member.

I believe that another problem in our churches is "underemployment" not just unemployment. Some people are inadequately employed because new ministries are not permitted to match their gifts, experience, passion or personality. This happens when an atmosphere of fear, lack of trust or tradition is pervasive in the church. When this exists we will have too many people gifted for one thing and working outside of the ministry for which they are gifted. This is unfruitful, frustrating, and wasteful.

The church can move to the next level in the area of participation by establishing structure in its leadership and cultivating an atmosphere of permission-giving. When this is done, the church allows members access to the functional operation of the body, consents to God's calling on the lives of its members and gives them license to fully participate in ministry. Paul says, "let him." If it's teaching, let him teach. If it's encouraging, let him encourage. If it's contributing, let him contribute. If it's helping, let him. If it's giving, let him!

---

[1] Senge, P.M. "The Fifth Discipline: The Art and Practice of the Learning Organization." New York, Doubleday, 1996.

Study Guide: Moving To Next Level Participation

1. What is your level of participation?

   Commitment

   Genuine Compliance

   Formal Compliance

   Grudging Compliance

   Noncompliance

   Apathy

2. The Apostle Paul urges us to move to a higher level of participation through _____, _____ and _____.

3. The purpose of the believer's body is to be the _____ and the _____ through which God accomplishes His works.

4. What do you need to do in order to move to the next level in your participation?

5. It takes the _____ of believers to produce the results God desires.

6. Without adequate participation in the work of the ministry, something will always go _____.

7. Believers must understand that we are to _____ our physical bodies and its use to the will of God.

8. The proper perspective is necessary for increasing levels of participation - a proper perspective of _____, other _____, and the importance of the _____.

9. Believers should view their gifts and abilities to serve in the church as _____.

10. What do the following scripture verses share about next level participation:

    1 Chronicles 4: 9-10

    1 Peter 4:10

Romans 6:13

11. Scripture Memory: Ephesians 2:10

8

Next Level Profession

Acts 1:8 NIV

8 But you will receive power when the Holy Spirit comes upon you; and you will be my witnesses in Jerusalem, and in all Judea and Samaria, and to the ends of the earth.

The growth of the body of Christ is inconceivable without believers sharing their faith with the unsaved, the untaught and the unchurched. We do almost everything associated with the Christian faith including worshipping, singing, preaching, teaching and giving. But when it comes to sharing our faith, many of us fall short. We are plainly taught in scripture that an active witness is to accompany our faith in Christ. *"You are witnesses of these things. I am going to send you what my Father has promised; but stay in the city until you have been clothed with power from on high" (Luke 24:48-49 NIV).*

What Is Next Level Profession?

Next level profession is the lifestyle of a believer under the anointing of the Holy Spirit who is consistently occupied in thought, word or deed in the declaration of their faith in Jesus Christ.

What Must Be Considered?

The Greek word for witnesses is "martus," which is the same word from which we derive the word "martyr" in the English language. A martyr is defined as "someone who sac-rifices his life for something of great value, for the sake of principle or devotion to a cause." Jesus says we will be His witnesses. In other words, we are to openly profess our belief in Jesus Christ. This profession is our duty. We typically think of our profession as our line of work, business, occupation, job or career. We define it in terms of our vocation and recognize that it may require advanced education and training, and the use of intellectual skills. Next level profession, as our Lord reveals in His Word, is openly participating in the active sharing of Christ as the disciple's primary function. As we seek the guidance of the Holy Spirit in choosing a ministry, it is important for us to understand who we are. Our involvement in ministry only furthers our opportunity to be witnesses. *"You did not choose me, but I chose you and appointed you to go and bear fruit - fruit that will last. Then the Father will give you whatever you ask in my name" (John 15:16 NIV).* Howbeit, we all know that we are employed in the corporate arena, but next level profession recognizes the believer's primary task as a witness of their faith in Jesus Christ.

God is faithful in that He not only

> *Next level profession, as our Lord reveals in His Word is openly participating in the active sharing of Christ as the disciple's primary function.*

> *God is faithful in that He not only calls us to be witnesses, but He also equips us for our task.*

calls us to be witnesses, but He also equips us for the task. Christ tells the disciples before His ascension in Luke 24:49 that they will receive power when the promised Holy Spirit is come upon them. We are each empowered by the Holy Spirit to be an effective witness. Next level profession is not humanly contrived or manufactured, but it is instead the direct result of God's work in us.

> *Next level profession is not humanly contrived or manufactured, but it is instead the direct result of God's work in us.*

If we desire to go to the next level in our profession of Jesus Christ, it is necessary for us to understand that being a witness precedes witnessing. Our primary concern should be to be a witness. Once you become a witness, you are burdened to witness. Being a witness necessitates witnessing. In other words, if you really are a witness, it's going to come out of you. *"For out of the overflow of the heart the mouth speaks" (Matthew 12:34b NIV).*

> *If we desire to go to the next level in our profession of Jesus Christ it is necessary for us to understand that "being a witness" precedes "witnessing."*

Once we understand that "being" necessitates "doing," we are compelled to open our mouths and minister to the lost. We will become burdened for the lost to come to Christ.

We need to be witnesses also because church growth has not managed to keep pace with the growth of the population in our communities. Each one of us knows someone who is not a part of the church or who has not accepted Christ. Consequently, we need to go to the next level in our profession. Image what Jesus sees every week when we fail to share our faith. We should not be going about our daily routine and never saying anything about our Lord and Savior. We shouldn't continue to enjoy the worship service Sunday after Sunday and never attempting to win anyone over to Christ.

Where Does God Want Me To Be?

We first need to be more loving if we're going to go to the next level in the profession of our faith. We have to care for one another. Love fosters unity. Love creates loyalty within the body of Christ. As we love each other, we will truly be identified with Jesus. Jesus says, *"A new command I give you: Love one another. As I have loved you, so you must love one another. By this all men will know that you are my disciples, if you love one another" (John 13:34-35 NIV).*

> *Love creates loyalty to one another and within the body of Christ.*

The second step to next level profession is to be filled. We must be filled with the Spirit of God. Too many believers are relying on their own abilities instead of God's infilling of the Holy Spirit. Filled means to cause to abound, to make complete. Whatever your defencies are, when you are filled with the Spirit, God makes up for the rest. He will make you complete. Too many of us in the church are full of other emotions like doubt, fear, worry, gossip, hatred and jealousy. Characteristics like these are the very reason we are not witnessing as we should. When you are filled with the Spirit, you will possess the boldness He gives. *"The wicked man flees though no one pursues, but the righteous are as bold as a lion" (Proverbs 28:1 NIV).*

Next level profession needs to be relational. Believers need to be able to relate to the unsaved. We need to be human in our testimonies. If we are going to gain the trust of an unbeliever, we must demonstrate a genuine interest in them and meet them where they are, at their point of need. Paul states, *"To the Jews I became like a Jew, to win the Jews. To those under the law I became like one under the law (though I myself am not under the law), so as to win those under the law. To those not having the law I became like one not having the law (though I am not free from God's law but am under*

Christ's law), so as to win those not having the law. To the weak I became weak, to win the weak. I have become all things to all men so that by all possible means I might save some" (1 Corinthians 9:20-22 NIV). Our attitudes have a profound impact on our witness. We can turn people away from the church if our behavior or presentation is judgmental or does not begin on their level.

Next level profession must be intentional. If we are going to win souls to Christ, it will not happen by accident. True disciples are deliberate and intentionally share their faith with others. As a matter of fact, we must look for opportunities to share our faith. When we go to work, next level profession recognizes that God has sent us there as a witness for Him. Consequently, we need to be wise in our attitude, speech and behavior. Without wisdom, we may respond inappropriately and misrepresent Christ. Our duty is to bear witness, but the danger always exists that we can bear false witness.

Next level profession must be steadfast. In spite of any opposition we may face, we need to hold fast to our profession of faith. We must grow beyond only being able to be secure in our profession when everything is going well. We have to hold fast in good times as well as rough times. By doing so, we develop a consistent witness. Anything other than a consistent witness will not help us to achieve next level profession.

Next level profession must be prepared. Preparation is more than just exercising the discipline of scripture memory. While it is good for the development of the believer, scripture memory does not completely prepare you to share your faith. We need to be prepared to share our faith and reasons why we believe what we do as God gives us the opportunity. We need to be prepared to the point that we can bring hope to a despairing situation. We need to be able to minister the message of Christ in any situation. In order to do this, we must give our responses some thought. We must have our answers prepared. Professionals take continuing education courses concerning their area of expertise and so should we.

Study Guide: Moving To Next Level Profession

1. Next level profession, as our Lord reveals in His Word is openly participating in the active sharing of Christ as the disciple's _____ function.

2. God is faithful in that He not only calls us to be witnesses, but He also _____ us for the task.

3. Steps Toward Next Level Profession:
   - a. _____ John 13:34
   - b. _____ Acts 4:8
   - c. _____ 1 Corinthians 9:22
   - d. _____ Colossians 4:6
   - e. _____ Hebrews 10:23
   - f. _____ 1 Peter 3:15

4. Our duty is to bear witness, but the danger always exists that we can bear _____ witness.

5. What do the following scripture verses share about next level profession?

   Acts 1:22

Acts 2:32

Matthew 28:19

Mark 16:15

Luke 24:46-49

John 15:27

6. Scripture Memory: Matthew 28:19-20

9

Next Level Prosperity

2 Corinthians 8:7 NIV

7 But just as you excel in everything, in faith, in speech, in knowledge, in complete earnestness and in your love for us, see that you also excel in this grace of giving.

Many of us in the church today want to excel in our spiritual development. We want to excel in our faith. We want to speak to the mountain and see it move. We want to excel in our utterance. We want to open our mouths and experience the power of God flowing freely to bless those around us. We want to excel in knowledge. We want to know more about God's Word. All of these desires are good. But the Apostle Paul encourages us that we also need to excel in the grace of giving. Not only are we to be the recipients of the abundant blessings of God, but we also are to have a balanced Christian life. We are to excel in our giving. We must not only be willing to personally prosper, but also to prosper others.

What Is Next Level Prosperity?

Next level prosperity is the relationship a believer can have with God wherein he trusts God's ability to provide for his needs and the needs of others. It's knowing that we have God's anointing on our lives no matter what happens.

What Must Be Considered?

If we are going to participate in next level prosperity, we need to overcome the hurdle of our wills. We must first recognize why we don't presently give? There are a few reasons we can rule out up front. It is not because of a lack of knowledge. We all are aware of existing needs in the church, community and those around us. We know of worthy causes that could benefit from our monetary contributions. We are also not short of justifiable reasons to give. Our churches are full of reasons why we need to give: youth ministry, Christian education, family ministry, missions, evangelism, the nursery, administration, buildings and much more. We also do not lack the opportunity to give. Each Sunday, members are given the opportunity to support the work of the church through tithes, offerings, sacrificial gifts and love offerings. A lack or shortage of money is more than likely the most popular reason many of us offer as to why we are not able to give as instructed in scripture. We make money that our fore parents didn't even dream about. Quite honestly, in many instances our only lack is what's left after waste and mismanagement.

Paul uses the example of the Macedonia church as an example of those who were without much, but willingly gave of their means. He tells the believers at Corinth that the Macedonians gave in the midst of their affliction. *"And now, brothers, we want you to know about the grace that God has given the Macedonian churches. Out of the most severe trial, their overflowing joy and their extreme poverty welled up in rich generosity" (2 Corinthians 8:1-2 NIV).* They had their share of problems, persecutions and afflictions, but these did not prevent them from participating in the faith through next level prosperity, trusting God to not only meet their needs but also the needs of others through them. And not only did they give, but Macedonia gave in spite of their affliction, with overflowing joy. Their faith was coupled with an overflowing joy.

The Lord would have us to recognize that by the godly example of the Macedonians that everybody has something to give regardless of their circumstances. So the limitation of our resources is not an acceptable reason for our lack of giving. Next level prosperity

> *The limitation of our resources is not an acceptable reason for our lack of giving.*

gives beyond one's apparent ability. In their extreme poverty, extreme generosity welled up in them. Like the Macedonians, we are to be rich in generosity.

The Macedonians weren't asked or pleaded with to give. They gave on their own. In fact, they insisted on giving. How many of us upon arriving to church after the collection has been taken on a Sunday morning, would find an usher, trustee or deacon and insist that our offering be added?

Paul records that the Macedonians, on their own, urgently pleaded for their gifts to be accepted. When was the last time we gave beyond our apparent ability?

Where Does God Want Me To Be?

What enables us to reach next level prosperity? **Of primary importance, Paul would have us to know that the Macedonians gave themselves first to the Lord.** The willingness to give of our possessions must be preceded by our making Jesus Christ the Lord of our lives.

> *The willingness to give of our possessions must be preceded by our making Jesus the Lord of our lives.*

Next level prosperity cannot be achieved as long as our minds are focused solely on receiving. Unfortunately, the problem with many contemporary churches today is that many of the people act like consumers. They shop for churches with which to unite. And when they find one that they feel meets their needs, they give themselves to everything in that church, but the Lord. They give themselves to the choir, the preacher, or the ministries. This is why they hold onto their money, because if they had given themselves to the Lord first, they would support whatever Jesus is doing in that church. They would not pick and choose. When Jesus is Lord, it means that

He is the Master and we are the slaves. The slave obeys the dictates of the Master. We must ask ourselves is Jesus Lord in my life including the area of my giving?

One of the benefits of this example set by the Macedonian church is that it gives us a living application of a spiritual truth. When we look at their example, our excuses becomes greatly limited. Thus, we are provided foundation in the Word of God that when we resolve in our hearts to give of our time, talents and finances, our resources should not solely dictate our decision to give. When we embrace the fact that giving is something that God wants us to do, we will do it in spite of our finances. We will no longer be hindered by our financial resources.

The example given by the Macedonians should only serve to seed our faith. We are admonished by the Apostle Paul, *"But just as you excel in everything - in faith, in speech, in knowledge, in complete earnestness and in your love for us - see that you also excel in this grace of giving," (2 Corinthians 8:7 NIV).* The exhortation comes from the man of God. The duty of God's anointed leaders is to challenge, teach, exhort, correct, rebuke and train in righteousness concerning the whole counsel of God, and that includes giving. We need to begin to thank God for a word from Him through His inspired messengers. We must stop treating sermons as if they are some exercise of gifts by men and women who merely like to talk. We must begin to see God working through His anointed leaders, by His Spirit, in an effort to try and get us to move to the next level. As we begin to see the promises of God unfold in our lives, a willingness to give will be produced, not guilt. The anointing that God gives His preachers and teachers is not to be used to manipulate His people. When conviction occurs, growth will occur as well. God's

> *As we begin to see the promises of God unfold in our lives, a willingness to give will be produced, not guilt.*

leaders should not have to resort to trickery or gimmicks in order to fabricate a willingness to give among the people of God. God is pleased and therefore sends prosperity when we give out of obedience instead of some other motivation.

Jesus Christ is our eminent example for giving. *"For you know the grace of our Lord Jesus Christ, that though he was rich, yet for your sakes he became poor, so that you through his poverty might become rich" (2 Corinthians 8:9 NIV).* For our sakes Jesus left His free and carnate riches to take on fleshly poverty. It was grace in operation. Paul says we are to be like Jesus. Ultimately, when believers understand what Jesus did for their personal salvation, they don't have to be coaxed or prodded to give. A willingness will swell up in our hearts to give and do what God has called for us to do. The benefit is that the believer personally decides to give without feeling pressure and with a cheerful disposition. We then have confidence that our gift is acceptable relative to what we have, not according to what we do not have. Paul's words teach us not to focus on numbers. Don't focus on numbers or guilt. Paul's encouragement to the church is liberal. God honors the believer's gift no matter the size or the timing when it comes from an eager heart. The benefit of an eager heart is when we become eager, God gets eager.

> *God honors the believer's gift no matter the size or the timing when it comes from an eager heart.*

Study Guide: Moving To Next Level Prosperity

1. Next level prosperity is the _____ a believer can
   have with God wherein he trusts God's ability to meet his
   needs and also the needs of others. It's having God's
   _____ no matter what.

2. We need to overcome the hurdle of our _____.

3. We can rule out the following reasons for our lack of giving:

         a. _____

         b. _____

         c. _____

         d. _____

4. The Macedonian church gave in the midst of their
   _____.

5. Next level prosperity gives _____ one's apparent
   ability.

6. The Macedonians gave themselves to the Lord

   _____.

7. The example given by the Macedonians should

   _____ our faith.

8. _____ is our eminent example for giving.

9. What do the following scriptures share about next level
   prosperity?

   2 Corinthians 9:6-7

   Proverbs 11:24-25

   Proverbs 22:9

   Galatians 6:7-10

10. Scripture Memory: Galatians 6:10

10

Next Level Provision

2 Corinthians 12:7-10 NIV

7 To keep me from becoming conceited because of these surpassingly great revelations, there was given me a thorn in my flesh, a messenger of Satan, to torment me.

8 Three times I pleaded with the Lord to take it away from me.

9 But he said to me, "My grace is sufficient for you, for my power is made perfect in weakness." Therefore I will boast all the more gladly about my weaknesses, so that Christ's power may rest on me.

10 That is why, for Christ's sake, I delight in weaknesses, in insults, in hardships, in persecutions, in difficulties. For when I am weak, then I am strong.

The Apostle Paul is a good model for us to refer to as we consider the different experiences that accompany our spiritual progression. We can learn a great deal from his life and testimony, which can prepare us in our expectations for the Christian walk.

Moving to the next level for a fully-developing follower of Christ is a spiritual objective that is progressive in nature. It is significant spiritual growth and development that draws you closer to God. It takes us higher and higher in development, maturity and experiences. Although His is a worthy goal for our lives, we have to realize that many will stay at the same level year after year because they are "afraid of heights." Every believer does not have the mindset of the Apostle Paul who wrote: *"Not that I have already obtained all this, or have already been made perfect, but I press on to take hold of that for which Christ Jesus took hold of me" (Philippians 3:12 NIV).*

What Is Next Level Provision?

Next level provision is the privilege of experiencing God's grace through the recognition of our weaknesses.

What Must Be Considered?

Paul shares with us the special privilege he experienced from God through visions and revelations. He was given the favor, honor and opportunity to see at a higher level. He received disclosures of truth and instruction from the mind of God concerning the unknown. Next level living permits one to receive special riches in the spiritual realm. Next level living is a privilege, is an opportunity to draw closer to Christ. The ability to converse with God through the discipline of prayer is a privilege. We cannot get caught up in the privilege of getting closer. Like Paul, we must refrain from the temptation to boast. Whenever we find ourselves bragging about what we have done for the Lord, this is an indication that we may have fallen victim to pride.

In light of the surpassing, great revelations Paul experienced, he states that he was given a thorn in his flesh so that he would not become conceited. *"The Lord detest all the proud of heart" (Proverbs 16:5).*

The privilege that Paul experienced had its price. As is the case with all believers, growth in the Lord carries a price. There will be some sacrifices and hardships that we will have to endure as a result of our mov-

Growth in the Lord carries a price.

ing to a new level. We may experience loss or hardship in varying forms. In the case of Paul, he says *"there was given me...a messenger of Satan to torment me."* The thorn was definitely something that frustrated him and caused trouble in his life. It was something that hurt and bothered him. The hindrances we experience are attempts to make us lose focus, namely of God's power. By focusing on our own limitations, we can quickly become defeated.

When we move up, there should be an expectation to experience pain and pressure on another level. We will have our personal thorns. There's a price involved as we move up. God wants us to know that no matter how high we move up, we are still human and completely dependent upon Him.

> *God wants us to know that no matter how high we move up, we are still human and completely dependent upon Him.*

Where Does God Want Me To Be?

As Paul learned as a result of his thorn, next level provision trusts God's provision for life's pain. The thorns of life weaken us. But grace, the next level provision of God, is His merciful kindness that endowed Paul with unfailing strength. It is His endowment of favor for the times of trouble. God's grace is also our divine provision in our times of weakness. *"I am not saying this because I am in need, for I have learned to be content whatever the circumstances. I know what it is to be in need, and I know what it is to have plenty. I have learned the secret of being content in any and every situation, whether well fed or hungry, whether living in plenty or in want. I can do all things through him who gives me strength" (Philippians 4:11-13 NIV).*

Grace was God's prescription for Paul's pain. Paul had a specific pain. He made a specific request for his specific pain, but God prescribed grace. Grace could handle Paul's specific problem. Because of God's grace, we are provided with unfailing strength to contend with pain. Although it is typical to want our thorns to be removed, God's provision of grace enables us to handle them. God's grace will help us to cope with any predicament.

As was the case with Paul, so it is with believers today, we are waging a battle between our desires and God's will. Paul prayed that the thorn would be removed, but God desired otherwise. Next level people want God's will over their own. Whatever predicament we find ourselves dealing with whether it is loneliness, sickness or financial hardship, God's grace may be His provision for our struggle, rather than the removal, cure, or deliverance from what pains us.

As a fully-developing follower of Christ, we must begin to take pleasure in God's provision because we know that it is sure. We can be assured of God's sustaining power through next level provision of His grace. He has already promised us that it will be sufficient. As a result, we are not to boast in our abilities, but rather, we must begin to recognize that it was because of our weakness that God's grace was provided. So instead, like the Apostle Paul, we are to boast in our weakness. Thus, God is glorified. He gets the glory. We cannot take any of the credit because we openly admit that we could not sustain ourselves through our trial. Next level people discover the joy of God's grace, the pleasure of pain, problems and pressure.

As we trust in next level provision, or the grace of God, we discover that:

God's NO doesn't mean NOTHING. When we pray and make our desires known to our heavenly Father, He doesn't always go along with our program. In fact, what God is really saying is that "The choice is mine, not yours." He may not give us what we ask for, not because He doesn't want us to have anything, but because He wants us to have the right thing. We can rejoice because He has already promised to meet our needs in Philippians 4:19. His provision is sure.

We should also experience joy when we learn that God's strength is available through our weakness. When Paul looked at his weakness and declared it to God, God's power would overcome him and he would be taken to a new level. In his declaration, Paul got his mind off of his torment and was instructed to focus on God's grace. When we go to God, we go as ourselves, in human weakness. But through the grace of God, He uses our weakness for His glory.

Growth comes through trials. Growth comes through trials because we pray differently when we are tried. We discover more about God when we seek Him in tough times. And as a result, we experience growth which ultimately causes us to rejoice. I am convinced that as we go through trials, we pray more fervently. Scripture records that fervent prayer produces much in the life of the believer. Thus, we experience our desired breakthrough and begin to rejoice that God's grace is sufficient.

Study Guide: Moving To Next Level Provision

1. Next level provision is the privilege of experiencing God's grace through the recognition of our _____.

2. Next level living permits one to receive the riches of the spiritual realm. As one moves us, there should be an awareness of the temptation to become _____.

3. Growth in the Lord carries a _____.

4. God wants us the know that no matter how high we move up, we are still human and completely _____ upon Him.

5. Next level provision trusts God's _____ for life's pain.

6. _____ was God's prescription for Paul's pain.

7. We are waging a battle between our _____ and God's will.

8. We must begin to take _____ in God's provision
   because we know that it is sure.

9. As we trust in next level provision, we discover that:

   a. _____

   b. _____

   c. _____

10. What do the following scriptures share about next level
    prosperity?
    Philippians 4:11-13

    2 Corinthians 13:4

    1 Peter 2:24

11. Scripture Memory: 2 Corinthians 12:9

11

The Next Level Play

The Next Level

By Teresa Corbett

("Moving On Up," sung to the tune of the theme song from The Jeffersons, opens up)

(Some people are standing and some are sitting. Eloise is serving something to drink. Mother Jeffrey is seated and refuses a drink. Flora is dusting.)

Georgio: You all know why I called this meeting.   I want to unveil something.

Thomas: Good Heavens, Georgio! Show some decency. *(covering Helena's eyes)* I see no just reason why you should be unveiling yourself.

Helena: I think he is talking about showing us a new idea.

Thomas: Oh! On second thought that could be worse. The last thing he unveiled was that NDK.

Helena: Yeah, the letters didn't even match the slogan: NDK - Making a Noticeable difference. Where's the logic in that?

Benson: *(dressed in African attire)* Thomas, do you think he noticed?

Georgio: Yeah, and I noticed you, too. How can I not

notice you when you are wearing every color known to man? You give the word "peacock" a whole new meaning.

Eloise: Georgio, we are here to talk about moving on up and not to pick on Benson. He's from the "Mother" country, Africa.

Georgio: Yeah, well, maybe it should be changed to the "Father" country. Then the colors would be more manly.

Benson: You really know how to color any situation, Mr. J?

Georgio: *(dismissing that statement)* On with the plan. *(unfolds chart of a complex, confusing drawing)* This is called "Next Level Commitment."

Flora: It looks like the next level commitment you need is to be committed to the next level of a mental institution...the point of no return level.

Mother Jeffery: Don't talk to my son like that. He's very intelligent. He is so mentally challenged...just like his mother.

Benson: That's not a good thing.

Georgio: *(jumps in)* I want each one of you to pick a card that represents getting to the next level: Tell me what you think it is. Then, I'll tell you the Master's plan.

Eloise: That would be you, Honey, the master.

Georgio: Yes, but not for this plan. You know our pastor says we are to follow God's plan. Now, read your card and tell me what you think. Flora, do you need me to read yours for you since you have problems reading?

Flora: No, I don't, but you can read my mind, my lips and my *(holds hands up to suggest fingering, but does not carry it out)*

Eloise: Flora!!!

Flora: *(sheepish grin as she realizes her inappropriate actions.)* *(quickly recovering)* Anyway, my card says, "Next Level Purity." I know this one. This card is for the Singles Ministry. You know what he told them not to do. You do remember, don't you?

Georgio: Flora, I told you that you needed help reading. Your card says "Next Level Peace."

Flora: *(looks at card again, realizes mistakes, grins awkwardly).*

Eloise: *(interrupting)* What Pastor wants us to know is that we all have to move to the next level of peace.

Georgio: Tell'um, Eloiseezie.

Eloise: The pastor told us that when peace prevails, situations are handled in a way that is just and right.

Flora: I agree 'cause just and right now I am retiring

from this meeting and going to relax in the purity of some peace and sleep.

Georgio: How are you going to move to the next level with that attitude? Why don't you expand your territory and make us some coffee?

Flora: Have you read your Bible lately? The Bible says, "He..brews," not "She..brews."

Helena: *(cuts in)* Let me read my card. It says, "Next Level Provision." That's easy.

Thomas: That's for the ministers on staff...and visiting preachers.

Georgio: and everybody in the church.

Eloise: Through prayer, God provides. Prayer changes things.

Flora: How come Mr. Jeffery is still the same?

Mother: Don't talk about my son like that? Prayer got him this far.

Flora: Well, prayer and the provision for a Greyhound bus need to take him back where he came from.

Eloise: To move to the next level, pastor reminded us that we had to not only pray for provision for ourselves, but we have to also pray for spiritual blessings, blessings that can benefit others, too.

Helena: Well, I never thought about that. We pray that God would provide cars, houses, jobs, and other things, but we don't think about how we can expand missions and use them for the glory of God.

Mother: Yes, that's why you should pick me up in that Lexus so that I won't have to take the Marta to come here.

Thomas: *(jumping in)* My card says, "Next Level Power." I am not sure that I know what this means.

Eloise: Think about if there were a power outage and we only had reserved power. That reserved power is not as potent and won't last forever. As Christians, we have a power supply that won't run out if we tap into that power the way it was intended to be.

Georgio: Jesus wants us to know that anyone who has faith in Him will do even greater things because he is going to the Father. Here is a promise of potential for the whole church body.

Thomas: So, in other words, we have the source to have real power in the spiritual sense that we don't tap into, but we fall all over ourselves trying to have wanna be power in the secular sense.

Benson: Like on your jobs down at AT&T, Atlanta Life, Kimberly-Clarke, the post office, the school system, the medical centers, the restaurant, the City, the State, the County, the wherever. You may wanna be in power, but you are only-gonna be limited in power. They control your level. But we are in control of how much power we can have in the spiritual sense; yet, we limit ourselves.

Georgio: Exactly!

Benson: Let's see what my card says. It says next level participation. I get it. With the next level of purity, the next level of praying, and the next level of power, we have to expand ministry through participation. We have to consider it our task to provide services to use our gifts to serve, to reach out, to be completely involved in the ministry.

Flora: What about the pastor? All he does is write sermons and fly all over the creation. Shouldn't he be the one to go out and do the ministering. And what about his wife? We should give her more to keep her busy. You know what they say, "Idle hands or an idle mind is the devil's workshop."

Georgio: God has given us all a purpose. The pastor and his wife are not expected to do everything, while we cruise. Do you know your purpose, your power, your participation level?

Eloise: *(towards audience)* We all participate, but at different levels. Some of us are at the near zero level. And then some of us participate, but not in a way that expands our level and allows us to make a noticeable difference.

Benson: So, whatever level we are at now, we can move up. We can participate and stop perpetrating.

(Characters are moved to get going to go the next level. They start gathering things. Joy of the revelation shows on each face. All except Georgio, who is pensive, prepare to leave.)

Georgio: Now, where is everybody going?

All: To the next level: *(to audience)* We want to see you there, too!

(theme song) (exit as theme song is played and sung)

Georgio: Hey, don't leave me!

-The End-

Props:

1. chart and easel

(a confusing drawing of Georgio's plan)

2. cards

(Write on a separate card for each of the following: Next Level Power, Next Level Provision, Next Level Participation, Next Level Commitment)

3. cups and pitcher

(coffee, water, or other beverage)

4. duster

5. Costumes:

Georgio (suit)

Eloise (nicely dressed)

Benson (African attire)

Flora (apron)

12

Study Guide Answer Key

Chapter 1 - Next Level Prayer

1. Jabez means **pain** or **sorrow**.

2. Next level prayer is a **choice**.

3. **Contentment**, or a lack of desire for change, will not produce next level results.

4. We must be careful not to look for **abundance** in the wrong places.

5. What are some of the false assumptions we make regarding the reason for the success others experience:
    a. **luck**
    b. **hard work**
    c. **long-study**
    d. **family**
    e. **friends**
    f. **money**
    g. **fate**

6. God wants you to:
    a. **prioritize** your spiritual development
    b. **request** the expansion of your boundaries
    c. **seek** additional influence
    d. **recognize** the sustaining power of God

Chapter 2 - Next Level Purity

1. Next level purity is not to be like the righteousness of the Scribes and Pharisees. It is NOT supposed to be:
    a. **external** (Luke 11:39)
    b. **burdensome** (Matthew 23:2-4)
    c. **selective** (Matthew 23:23)
    d. **self-exalting** (Luke 18:11)
    e. **hypocritical** (Mark 7:6)
    f. **negative** (Mark 2:24)

2. It is more important to be **reconciled** with others than to participate in religious duties.

3. Next level purity:
    a. **reverences life**
    b. **is committed to marriage and family**
    c. **is honest**
    d. **accepts suffering**
    e. **involves sacrificial love**

4. **Purity** begins with faith in Jesus Christ.

5. As we experience more of Christ in our lives, we are to practice **humility**.

6. We are to be active in **living** the Word of God.

7. We need to **empathize** with others.

8. Believers need to always practice **repentence**.

9. The Word of God is **intended** to be more than a forty-five minute sermon we experience each Sunday.

10. Part of what makes our **witness** effective is our ability to empathize with those who do not know Christ as their personal Lord and Savior.

11. The test of our righteousness is if we can love those who **dislike** us, hate us, and even try and hurt us.

Chapter 3 - Next Level Power

1. Next level power is available to **every** believer.

2. We were never intended to operate in the body of Christ on anything **less** than the power He provides in the person of the Holy Spirit.

3. We **cannot** be true Christians without the aid of the Holy Spirit.

4. Believers are to experience **greater** degrees of great-ness, or the "greater works," in their ministries.

5. We must have **faith** in the work of Christ before the cross, on the cross and after the cross.

7. Not only is the believer to read and obey the Word of God, but also the **voice** of the Holy Spirit.

Chapter 4 - Next Level Peace

1. We fail to have peace because of:
    a. **parental upbringing**
    b. **environment**
    c. **authority figures**
    d. **past or present crisis**
    e. **emotions**

2. Many of God's children have been living on a **piece-meal** instead of the "great peace" spoken of by the psalmist.

3. While we must practice patience with others, we must also be patient with **God**.

4. There can be no peace without **prayer**.

5. The extent of our **persuasion** in God's ability to answer our request must be evident in our prayers.

6. Next level peace is **patient**.

7. Next level peace prays:
    a. **thankfully**
    b. **positively**
    c. **persistently**
    d. **purposefully**

Chapter 5 - Next Corporate Level Peace

1. The Greek word for peace, eirene, describes harmonious **relationships** between men, between nations, between God and man, freedom from outside intrusion and a sense of contentment.

2. When people come to the campus of the local church, they should sense the manifestation of **peace**.

3. We cannot have peace in the local church when people live, think and behave in opposition to God's **Word**.

4. There should be a "zero tolerance policy" against **intolerance**.

5. Next level peace occurs in the local church when members allow peace to **umpire** their thoughts, intentions, communication, facial expressions, mannerisms and the like.

6. Community is talking, listening, caring, knowing, serving, giving, in essence **relating**.

7. A **congregation** should be a living, functioning community.

8. Peace is dependent upon us taking **off** some stuff.

9. Peace in relationships and interaction among members requires us not just to put off but also to put **on**.

10. Believers in the church also need to put **up** with one another.

11. Peace is a **personal** responsibility before it becomes a corporate responsibility.

Chapter 6 - Next Level Praise

1. Next level praise is **continuous**!

2. Next level praise is not solely established for a **special group**.

3. Next level praise is not relegated to **specific circumstance**.

4. Next level praise is offered through **Christ**, with Christ on the mind and heart of the believer.

5. The Jews of the Old Testament were always required to bring some type of sacrifice when they worshipped God. A sacrifice was an offering or giving up of something precious and of value. The act was inconvenient, but done with a **willing** heart.

6. In the Old Testament, there were different types of sacrifices:
   a. **burnt offerings**
   b. **peace offering**
   c. **sin offering**
   d. **trespass offering**

7. Next level praise is **verbal**.

8. Next level praise is **effectual**.

Chapter 7 - Next Level Participation

2. The Apostle Paul urges us to move to a higher level of participation through **purpose**, **perspective** and **permission**.

3. The purpose of the believer's body is to be the **the temple of the Holy Spirit** and the **instrument** through which God accomplishes His works.

5. It takes the **combined** efforts of believers to produce the results God desires.

6. Without adequate participation in the work of the ministry, something will always go **lacking**.

7. Believers must understand that we are to **submit** our physical bodies and its use to the will of God.

8. The proper perspective is necessary for increasing levels of participation - a proper perspective of **oneself**, other **members**, and the importance of the **church**.

9. Believers should view their gifts and abilities to serve in the church as **privileges**.

Chapter 8 - Next Level Profession

1. Next level profession, as our Lord reveals in His Word is openly participating in the active sharing of Christ as the disciple's **primary** function.

2. God is faithful in that He not only calls us to be witness, but He also **equips** us for our task.

•

3. Steps Toward Next Level Profession:
   a. **Be loving** (John 13:34)
   b. **Be filled** (Acts 4:8)
   c. **Be relational** (1 Corinthians 9:22)
   d. **Be intentional** (Colossians 4:6)
   e. **Be steadfast** (Hebrews 10:23)
   f. **Be prepared** (1 Peter 3:15)

4. Our duty is to bear witness, but the danger always exists that we can bear **false** witness.

Chapter 9 - Next Level Prosperity

1. Next level prosperity is the **relationship** a believer can have with God wherein he trusts God's ability to meet his needs and also the needs of others. It's having God's **anointing** no matter what.

2. We need to overcome the hurdle of our **wills**.

3. We can rule out the following reasons for our lack of giving:
   a. **A lack of knowledge**
   b. **A good reason**
   c. **A lack of opportunity**
   d. **A lack of money**

4. The Macedonian church gave in the midst of their **affliction**.

5. Next level prosperity gives **beyond** one's apparent ability.

6. The Macedonians gave themselves to the Lord **first**.

7. The example given by the Macedonians should **seed** our faith.

8. **Jesus Christ** is our eminent example for giving.

Chapter 10 - Next Level Provision

1. Next level provision is the privilege of experiencing God's grace through the recognition of our **weaknesses**.

2. Next level living permits one to receive the riches of the spiritual realm. As one moves up, there should be an awareness of the temptation to become **conceited**.

3. Growth in the Lord carries a **price**.

4. God wants us the know that no matter how high we move up, we are still human and completely **dependent** upon Him.

5. Next level provision trusts God's **provision** for life's pain.

6. **Grace** was God's prescription for Paul's pain.

7. We are waging a battle between our **desires** and God's will.

8. We must begin to take **pleasure** in God's provision because we know that it is sure.

9. As we trust in next level provision, we discover that:
    a. **God's NO doesn't mean nothing**
    b. **We should experience joy when we learn that God's strength is available to us through our weaknesses**
    c. **Growth comes through trials**

Epilogue

There is a tremendous danger in not moving to the next level. The danger exists for an individual, group, ministry, or church. Stagnation is so common in the religious realm. We say that the church is a living organism and that the born again believer has new life in Christ. Living things must grow. They must change or death is certain.

Discipleship is a progressive journey. There's always something more to learn, experience, do, plan, pray for, stand for or against, and share. God calls us to a fresh and higher encounter with Him. Therefore, believers must avoid stagnation. We must guard against complacency, apathy, self-righteousness, pride, or satisfaction. God constantly calls upward. You may now be wondering: How do I get started? What steps do I take to move to the next level in my praying, purity, power, praise, peace, participation, prosperity, and provision? I suggest the following steps to get started.

Evaluate your personal walk with God. Prayerfully discover your strengths and weaknesses. How much time do you spend with the Lord? Have you overextended yourself in ministry? Have you slacked up in ministry? Are you spiritually stronger this year than last? Can your pastor depend on you? Do you know your spiritual gift or gifts? How do you approach worship each week? What is your relationship like with your family? Can anyone sense God's hand on your life? Are you stuck in tradition, rituals, and ceremonies? Can you lead someone to Christ? Do you share Christ regularly?

Develop a personal mission statement. Write a statement that expresses what you understand to be God's purpose for you in life. It should point out what is vitally important to you and provide direction for your future goals. This statement will allow you to check your progress toward your life's mission. In writing, it would be good to think about what you would want said at your retirement or as a eulogy. Here's a sample:

Mission Statement
My mission in life is to be a leader,
a person who influences others for good.
To live my life as a life-long learner,
always aware that God's Word is inexhaustible.
To love and lead my family,
knowing that leadership begins a home.
To dedicate my life to others,
helping them to find their Divine purpose in life.

Eliminate everything and everyone from holding you back. You must be willing and determined to leave whatever keeps you at your present level. Sometimes it's a habit. Sometimes it's a person. Sometimes it's a place or position. Whatever it is, if God is calling, you need to leave. What's before you is worth much more than what you leave.